18 Folgate Street

DENNIS SEVERS

Explains some of its mysteries . . . halfway

DENNIS SEVERS

18 FOLGATE STREET

The Tale of A House in Spitalfields

WITH AN INTRODUCTION

BY

Peter Ackroyd

Photographs by M. Stacey Shaffer

VINTAGE
and
Chatto & Windus
LONDON

Published by Chatto & Windus 2001
Vintage 2002

2 4 6 8 10 9 7 5 3

First published in Great Britain in 2001 by Chatto & Windus
Random House, 20 Vauxhall Bridge Road, London sw1v 2sa

Addresses for companies within The
Random House Group Limited can be
found at: www.randomhouse.co.uk/offices.htm

The Random House Group Limited Reg. No. 954009
www.randomhouse.co.uk

A CIP catalogue record for this book is available from the British Library

isbn 0701172797 hardback
isbn 0099437368 paperback

The Random House Group Limited supports The Forest Stewardship
Council (FSC), the leading international forest certification organisation.
All our titles that printed on Greenpeace approved FSC certified paper
carry the FSC logo. Our paper procurement policy can be found at
www.rbooks.co.uk/environment

Set in 12 on 17pt Garamond
Designed by Peter Ward

All photographs © M. Stacey Shaffer
Endpaper drawings by James Howett

Printed and bound in China by C&C Offset Printing Co., Ltd

CONTENTS

INTRODUCTION

The strange journey of Dennis Severs, who died in December 1999 at the age of fifty one, began when as a child in Southern California he discovered in books and photographs the quality of what he called 'English light'. It was somehow warmer and richer than the clearer and dryer light he knew closer to home, and he followed it inevitably and ineluctably until it brought him to a narrow street in Spitalfields several years later. Here the house, 18 Folgate Street, finally found him. As he explains at one point in this mysterious and fascinating memoir, he had, without knowing, 'been collecting the contents' of this dwelling ever since he was eighteen years old. So the house called to him, and he responded. Of course he had to purchase it, rackety and rundown as it was, but before he began the process of restoration he had to learn its secrets. He slept in each of its ten rooms so that he might acquire their 'aura' or 'atmosphere', and he discovered that only certain objects would 'fit' within them. He was amassing 'signposts to the thinking of other times', and by an extraordinary act of intuition or empathy was able to feel their collective presence. He recreated the outlines of the past, which then surrounded the visitors who came to the house in large numbers.

In that sense it can hardly be coincidence that the house was located in Spitalfields, because of all London areas it is perhaps the one most powerfully haunted by intimations of its past. It is the area of notorious darkness – Sweeney Todd was born close to Folgate Street, and the entire area was once dominated by the brief but infamous career of Jack the Ripper – but it has also been an area which has harboured strangers like Dennis Severs himself. In turn the Huguenots, the Jews and the Muslim Bengalis have made it their home. But it is a district whose history has now become, literally, an open secret. Recent excavations beside Spitalfields Market have revealed the various strata of London from the fourth century onwards. So Dennis Severs had found a welcoming area for his own experiment in recovering past time.

The house was to recover its origins, in other words, and he set out to furnish and ornament its rooms so that it became a living image of the eighteenth-century house which it once had been. It had its own life and personality, which Dennis Severs felt compelled to revive and maintain. He even created an imaginary family, the Gervais or Jervis family, who would occupy the rooms and thus become the embodiment or shape of the house's spirit. So he began in the cellar, the heart of darkness, where there were the scattered remains of an old hospice and leper hospital. Next to it was the kitchen, and Severs delighted in the contrast between light and shadow, welcoming warmth and chill despair. There would have been Saxon Londoners in the vicinity, and perhaps even the long dead spoke to him; he seems to have been inspired by an Anglo-Saxon vision of the world.

But Severs was also a novelist and a romancer. The house became a living story, with each of its rooms as a separate chapter. His narrative itself leads the readers forward so that they feel as if they are beside him, listening to his voice and following the direction of his gaze. There are times when he lends a material and tactile quality to the adventure so that it leaves the head and enters the body: 'Apply your hands to both sides of the door; crack them open at the centre, and then gently, very gently, push back both sides.' What will you see, then, when the door is opened? It is a gate, a pathway, into another time. But so great is the immersion in this experience that the reader (and of course the visitor) becomes a character in the house's story. 'As an artist,' he writes, 'my canvas is your imagination'; by which he means that it is only in the private communing of each reader that the past can truly be said to live. It becomes 'an adventure of the imagination' with no boundaries.

This book is also about 'the space between', the air between objects which becomes charged with their presence, that intangible and ineffable 'aura' which holds being together in its capacious embrace. He describes it as 'a baroque painting, in three dimensions' but it provides more the effect of a still life. Note, however, that the life is only still, not absent. The house in Folgate Street is not a museum piece but a living thing; it is a revenant, a retrieval, with its own laws of growth and change. As Dennis Severs used to say to his visitors, 'You either see it, or you don't.' Those who 'see' it are unequivocally blessed.

Here a whole past comes alive in the most minute detail; there are sound effects and physical effects so that the manner in which a man coughs, or a woman sits down on a high-backed chair, are clues to an entire civilisation. The shape of an overturned glass or half-eaten apple may intimate the contours of the past more accurately than any historical or sociological study. Yet if the past returns to us then, in that same movement of sensibility, we may return to the past. To the visitors he explained that 'we have only to travel in Time to find that one part of us or the other, has already got there and made itself the better part of an Age'. In the experience of looking backward we may see images of our own selves, and the exploration of an ancient house also becomes the exploration of our own psyche. It has often been claimed that each house has its own personality, and Dennis Severs's book sustains that theme throughout, but what if the house adopted the personality of those who walked within it? These are some of the mysteries which may be derived from his text.

When he introduces the visitors to the drawing room, they find themselves framed in the mirror by an eighteenth-century interior; they are part of that interior, so that 'from you everything in your sight begins, just as everything in your sight returns to you'. There may be great philosophical questions here, concerning memory and perception, but the experience itself is intimate if unfamiliar. It may also be unnerving, since the past may return in order to claim those from the present. When the reader and the visitor stand in the bedroom of Mr and Mrs Jervis, as it were at their most private ceremonies, the eighteenth-century couple provide an almost conspiratorial welcome. 'No longer are they our Mr and Mrs Jervis,' Dennis Severs writes, 'now we are theirs.' The experience of the past can be so immediate and overwhelming, in such a context, that it seems literally to blot out the present.

In those novels of time travel, which were so popular at the turn of the nineteenth century, the fear is of being marooned in some alien and distant century. It represented the fear of 'the Other', and any alert reader will receive a presentiment of that fear while reading this book. It has been recorded, of course, that many of Severs's visitors became afraid. Indeed Severs seems to have provoked such reactions. He would place seashells under the carpets so that the unwary visitors feel that they have touched something hard and impenetrable; he fashioned a door without a latch which would suddenly swing open if anyone leaned against it. In a house which on one level was contrived to suggest the intimacy and familiarity of past times, this was a way of recovering their strangeness.

This narrative resembles a prose poem in celebration of time and history, but one that contains many kinds of aside and diversion; there are disquisitions on the cultural significance of the square and the circle, with revelations on the etymology of 'limp' and the obsessions with 'doubleness' in eighteenth-century aesthetics. So it is sober history as much as imaginative threnody; in fact it would not be going too far to state that a student of the period will learn as much from this book as from any more sober treatise. The journey through the house becomes a journey through time; with its small rooms and hidden corridors, its whispered asides and sudden revelations, it resembles a pilgrimage through life itself.

PETER ACKROYD, 2001

There are several people whom Dennis would have wished to thank, above all his late partner, Simon Pettet, whose eighteenth-century shoes star in one illustration and Isobel Barker, whose stories of the old East End inspired him. He would have loved Peter Ackroyd's introduction. Dennis's niece Stacey Shaffer took all the photographs, using the natural light he insisted on; Dan Cruickshank stepped into the author's place, checking the text and providing advice; Jim Howett drew the detailed end-papers; and Peter Ward designed the book including Dennis's own collages, rough drawings and captions. Mick Pedroli has looked after the house itself, and has been a constant resource. Thanks are also due to Lady Sarah Bagge; to Douglas Blain, Gareth Harris, Marianna Kennedy, David Milne, Martin and Monica Lane and Alan Williams for the Spitalfields Trust; to Tony Whittome, with whom Dennis first discussed publication; and to all his friends and neighbours in Spitalfields. It has been a privilege to be his editor.

JENNY UGLOW

'You either see it or you don't'

PROLOGUE

The only problem with living inside a painting is the messy business of getting in and out of that wretched frame.

For almost twenty years now visitors to this house have watched me light a candle in a dark cellar and lift it to an empty frame. Then, after I catch their eyes, they see me pass the candle through the frame and out the other side. I say, *'You see . . . I am going to take you through the frame and into a number of historic, but* inhabited *pictures: ones with a life and a reality of their own.'* Staring at the light, I make the candle move in circles — sometimes blowing at it — to tease the flame. *'And once I get you in there'*, with my voice now solidly from the other side, *'I am going to bombard all your senses – as Time itself would have – until'*, and I slowly pull the candle out of the frame, *'I create in your mind'*, and I nod, *'a "picture", or an impression – like a memory, which you will take away within you, and I hope keep for a very, very long time.'*

Inside that frame is where I live and taking people in there is how I make my living.

The day when I had to stop playing with the neighbourhood gang to step through the frame and start attending school was a bleak one. My question to my mother in the car on the way to my first day of kindergarten was, *'When do I get back?'* From then on, my freedom was compromised and my various schools began the task of trying to place me. I remember hearing that I lay somewhere in the region between 'exceptional' and 'mentally retarded', and the first months of each new school year seemed to be spent in being transported between different levels, teachers and classrooms, and at one stage even backwards in years.

A story began to circulate that the teachers were drawing lots: the loser took me on. In my last months at senior high school, when serious exams were imminent, I was finally awarded a tiny classroom to myself, something thought best for all. With no real category, my youth was spent in *the space between*: something to which I was always contentedly – if not happily – resigned. Besides, the views from there were exceptional; I became fascinated by the interplay – *between*.

As my colleagues' minds began to be distracted by education, I would drum up a colourful campaign of classroom disturbances to ensure that they would not leave me too far behind. Tossing spit wads and launching pencils into the depths of large Sixties bouffant hair-dos were my particular fortes. The 'October Uprising' got me banned from art classes, and the traffic chaos created by the state funeral I organised for a blackbird made the police watch me with suspicion. The latter was not my fault: drivers are reluctant to mow down thirty mourning children processing – with flowers – in a stately half-step. During peaceful interludes, I would lift my head to look out of the window and let my imagination travel out to other places and other times. On rainy days, when children were kept indoors without a break, one teacher would employ my imagination by sending me around to tell stories in an attempt to keep the peace. I would open up and share the adventures that went on inside my head; stories which I never had any trouble inventing, even as I spoke. I was troubled when, upon tiring, I tried to hand the story over to someone else, only to find that they were unable to continue it. Mystified, I would often feel that there was some contempt in this, and from the experience I developed a tendency to pick on those whose pigeonholed style of intelligence stifled their natural freedom to create. I still do.

My father loved the great outdoors and would sometimes plonk me in one of those still unrestored ghost towns in the American West while he went fishing. In California I can remember rolling a barrel from house to house in my baggy blue jeans in order to stand high enough to peek in windows. Then, if I spied something in a particular room – like a bottle of ink spilled over a turkey carpet – I would compose a story to explain it.

I built my first house at the age of four. At the same age I began collecting things, and I can well remember the time when a teacher who watched me picking things up in the school playground made me empty my pockets to share what I'd found with the rest of the class. I remember too how the entire class encircled me as I was forced to explain how the wooden eucalyptus twig was immediately (or, at least for me) recognisable as Charles de Gaulle. I precociously,

3

and perhaps defensively, took the subject on from de Gaulle's profile to French noses in general, and from the French nose to the nasal quality in their voices and accents. Of course that led to the nation's reputation for eating snails and frog's legs and a tradition of food based – not like ours, on filling the gut with gross amounts of anything fashion tells us is 'healthy' – but on a developed appreciation, or sensitivity, to taste. After all, taste *is* all related to the nose. However, what I remember most strongly was that the whole of the class – rough or smooth, smart or simple, Mexican or American – was in a mood to be taught about France.

Television ran old movies in the afternoons after school and became my babysitter. Through old black and white adaptations of Charles Dickens's stories, and *My Cousin Rachel*, came a tasty vision of England. My interest in paintings and films always remained pedestrian and was certainly never used as a form of escapism – except for little detours. I couldn't give a fig about brush strokes or technique, movie stars or directors, and am still embarrassingly ignorant as to any great names. I guess I sought old films as windows, where I saw life set in locations which were so different from that very clear, almost bleached, light that David Hockney captures in my own southern California. Down deep, I always believed that a day would come when I would travel past picture frames and into the marinated glow of a warmer, mellower and a more romantic light. There was one such light, in particular, that I saw in the combination of old varnish and paint, that appealed to me as my ideal. By the age of eleven it was identified as *English*.

As the Sixties approached, passion began to make me grow restless – like so many others of my age. It was a time when young people with dreams were applauded for setting out in search of them, and I began to resent the picture frames that stood between

4

me and the more interesting realities which I sensed were out there waiting. At the age of fifteen the quest was launched to locate that light – and, if I liked it, even move into it. With the money from my after-school paper rounds, washing dishes in restaurants in the early hours, and by not eating in order to save my lunch money, I was able to come to England to find it. I first visited in 1965, and then again in the following year, and finally I came here to live just five days after graduating from high school in 1967. It was love at first sight. I was eighteen.

I set out in search of the atmospheres that I had craved for and which I found. When I came back to school after my first two visits, something odd developed: I found myself able to assimilate what I was being taught. Away from my peer group and out in the world, sitting at tables with older people, and listening to what the real world needed to discuss, I had suddenly been able to perceive the reason for my education. A sense of relevance and structure began to develop which made me beg for more. I was inspired.

Once I settled in England I began to crave a home of my own. My collecting things began as a sport, but always to that end. Soon I was combing all the early morning street markets in London, and later the salesrooms too. Certain dealers sensed that I was looking for more than antiques and bric-a-brac, and always asked me to explain what it was – with so little money – I had found. For I was collecting *auras*: signposts to the thinking of other times. I would often stop and begin staring at an object on a stall and, as the dealer kept lowering his price, I would be thinking to myself, *Why did this once sell? So ugly . . . so fine . . . what, once, was its appeal?* Anything I bought became the centrepiece to my perception of a time in the history of my new homeland, around which I would then arrange the collected fruits of my curiosity. (All at bottom price!)

As time went on I began to see the shape of a bottle or a milk jug of a particular period as having the same general outline as that age's fashion and design. And by its similarities to other objects – including architecture and music – I could eventually work out what the *mood* was that once related them all: the spell which once constituted an 'age'. From there I would assimilate what I heard of real history: politics, legislation, battles, dates and so on. Again, for me, everything had to be related, and what little I do know about English history, I know this way. I can only dig into the air for the core of a subject and then work outwards from there. Human nature first, history later, as proof. I call it working *inside out*.

All this was put to work when, in 1969, I acquired a horse-drawn carriage to take people into the back streets of west London, to use its quiet squares and mews as the backdrop for what social history I knew and had arranged into a story. The atmosphere of these backwaters, with the clip-clop of the horse and carriage, worked as a time machine, and I was soon beginning to speak in the 'dramatic present', as if things in the past were happening right now. The combination worked astonishingly well, with people returning years later to say that they felt they had been on another planet while in the centre of their own city.

All this has led to my life and work at 18 Folgate Street. I bought the house in 1979 – not so much to restore as to bring it to life as my home. With a candle, a chamber pot and a bedroll, I began sleeping in each of the house's ten rooms so that I could arouse my intuition in the quest for each room's soul. Then, having neared it, I worked *inside out* to create what turned out to be a collection of atmospheres: moods that harbour the light and the spirit of various ages. As things came even closer together I began to realise that the material things I had been collecting all my life were really a cast of characters; and that 18 Folgate Street was destined to be their stage.

Sadly, I have recently come to accept what I refused to accept for so long: that the house may be only ephemeral.* This account is therefore intended to explain an old house that has become a famous time machine. On some magical nights it actually succeeds in drawing human nature and history together as one. So here, in a book, is one such night.

---

* Shortly before his death Dennis bequeathed the house and its contents to the Spitalfields Trust, which has agreed to run it as he intended. The house is still open to the public and people who knew Dennis well are keeping its spirit alive.

Out and In — This House and Your Senses

BEGINNING
ANOTHER TIME

From where you stand in Folgate Street you hear a door being unlocked from inside. As it opens you should remind yourself of the FOUR DIMENSIONS. The FIRST dimension is back and forth – the SECOND is up and down; both – like the door itself – are *flat*. The THIRD dimension is not flat, but comes forward and goes back to constitute a *space between*. Within it life happens. The door is opened, but now you hesitate. The *third* dimension before you contains something more than space: as thick as treacle – it hosts a foreign fourth. And the FOURTH dimension, dear Reader, is *Time*. So into Another Time . . . you go.

CHAPTER ONE

AT LIBERTY

If anywhere, it would have to happen here. ¶ At the time of my arrival at this address I was the only person in the street, and it was the darkness that exposed how very alone I was. Around me there were mainly warehouses — abandoned at nightfall — and the remaining town houses were by now boarded up and empty. Street lamps delivered amber patches — each one, with its beaten post, standing at its own silly angle. That light revealed stone streets with kerbs worn smooth by centuries of commercial traffic — the wear of which would glisten in the damp night air. An uncomfortable smell of market refuse lingered on with the afternoon and waited to join the evening one, wafted up with the warmth of the drains. In the distance – always – was the sound of a train or an unanswered burglar alarm clanging relentlessly out into an ominous gloom. With the view of the market from my back windows I could see a nightly installation performed by homeless tramps – who in long and blackened greatcoats stood holding bottles in a trance around one of the market's two eternally smouldering bonfires: I named the tableau *The Burghers of Calais*. An eerie spell reigned, which any newcomer quickly associated with Jack the Ripper. All the inhabitants who once thronged these streets were by now gone; I was alone: I was free.

With this as the stage, and with no television, anyone and everything on it could be viewed as theatre. I woke on my first morning to walk around the corner and find a tramp impaled on the railings of a house in Elder Street. He had fallen from a window while reaching down to strip the porch of its lead roof, all for the little bit of change it would give him to buy more drink. The sound of cats fighting rats had to be investigated, for it was missing in my education. And I remember thinking how presumptuous it was of me to get ready to answer the door – only because the pitch and tone of a sneeze out in the street was so distinctly middle class.

In the early hours of my first Monday morning, the sights and sounds of the opening scene of *My Fair Lady* awakened me: market barrows of vegetables and flowers being carted past my door; bonfires; shouts in Essex-Cockney English; even a few good punch-ups, all right outside. I realised that I only knew Spitalfields Market by name, and had somehow never caught it before it was locked up and tidied away. So, with only a minute black kitten named 'Whitechapel' inside, and *My Fair Lady* outside, I began my quest for a . . . home.

Now, if anywhere – it would have to happen here. Do you

remember how when still a child you were sometimes free to run loose in a field and romp: with nothing to break and no limits to noise? Folgate Street stands in the ancient Liberty of Norton Folgate, Bishopsgate Without, Spitalfields. The word *liberty* and *without*, when applied to ancient English place names implied that certain freedoms were associated with a region which sat outside the boundaries of a city or church's jurisdiction. Unorthodox beliefs and lifestyles were attracted to Spitalfields and settled here in the same quest for liberty.

If you have worn a suit for tonight's adventure, then what was until recently shabby Folgate Street might make you feel overdressed. Whereas – when still over the boundary of the City in Bishopsgate – you might have felt inappropriately attired in anything less. *Without* the Bishop's Gate in London Wall a loosened sense of liberty prevails, which contrasts sharply with so rigid and regimented a place as the City of London – *within*.

Being outside and extreme is what Spitalfields is all about. In medieval times the area was occupied by two classic categories of outcasts: the lepers and the insane, and Spitalfields derives its name from the leper hospice, St Mary's Spital and the fields on which it stood. The insane were taken out to the gates of St Mary's of Bethlehem or 'Bedlam', which occupied the site of what is today Liverpool Street Station.

Names such as Whitechapel, Calvin, Wesley, Worship, Tabernacle and Quaker Streets tell us that the Liberty attracted those who craved religious freedom, or *nonconformity*. French names like Nante Passage, Fournier, Fleur-de-Lys, French Place and Princelet Streets were given to other streets, showing how some of the people here had once come from a foreign land, the Huguenots, French Protestants. Fashion Street, Silk Street, Loom Court, Shuttle and Mulberry Streets along with pub names like the Crown and Shuttle and the Weaver's

Arms might also suggest the prominence of a silk or textile trade. Chance Street paints its own picture. You see, Reader, there must be a story in all this: something somewhere . . . in between?

By the early eighteenth century the City's ancient walls had burst and the last of the fields been built over to become London's first suburbs. Another natural human desire – for more light, cleaner and fresher air – attracted the City merchants out in the direction of a rural life suggested by other street names around us now, Blossom, Elder and Primrose. Certainly more attractive than the old City names from which they fled: Bread Street, Poultry, Cheapside, or Pudding Lane – where merchants were still cooped up in the 'shambles', living above their shops. New houses built of rich red brick with uniform white-painted window frames and door cases were now lining wider, lighter and straighter streets. A clean slate. And it is in one such early Georgian street that I now imagine you, my visitor, to stand.

Two pubs in Bishopsgate, the Sir Paul Pinder (now demolished) and Dirty Dick's, were both descended from private houses, with stories and legends attached to them. Dirty Dick was a silk master who, like Miss Havisham in Charles Dickens's *Great Expectations*, was jilted on his wedding day, and left the house untouched and dirty until the day he died. The façade of Paul Pinder's house is today preserved within the Victoria and Albert Museum.

People come to stand and stare up at 18 Folgate Street all through the day, and sometimes right into the night. Some do so in silence, while others try to explain its effect. Until tonight nobody has really done so.

It is time. You should face the door of the house and read the entry in a late nineteenth-century guidebook, printed on the back of the evening's instructions, which warns you not to speak.

16

Once the homes of prosperous master silk weavers, many of French Protestant or Huguenot origin, the houses in and around Spital Square are more reminiscent of Bloomsbury than they are of the East End . . . the area retains a curious atmosphere which no amount of rebuilding seems able to erase. In so much urban darkness a visitor might easily imagine turning a corner to find one of those old-time silk merchants – in knee-breeches and hose, wig and tricorne – and with a quantity of the stuff tucked under one arm – just dashing through one of those fine old door cases and off into another time.

You can hear the door of No. 18 being unlocked from inside. I should remind you that there are *four* dimensions, and that the fourth dimension is Time. Push open the door. There, in the air before you – in the space between things – is Another Time. Now it waits. What will happen to you will have to happen there. Enter.

Your guide tonight is a human instinct
. . . the one that leads you in the
direction of light and warmth.

CHAPTER TWO

RETURNING TO YOUR SENSES

Though dimensions may be seen as straight lines of direction, a visit to this old house defies such things by taking you on what might be compared to a carousel ride. Though its spinning, its music and pace, might at first make you mock and laugh – up and down – round and round – you are certain to fall under its spell by the time that you glide serenely to a halt. ¶ The first twirling shake-up is one of light. The difference of the old light in this house will reintroduce you to instincts and senses with which you were born, but which your education, etiquette and modern pampering have robbed you of. The crooked panels along both sides of the walls are covered in thick coats of cream gloss paint (generations of it) and lit only by the light of a few candles. You can see why so many Londoners went on using this colour for so long, in that it reflects and warms up what little light is available. Around you pitch-black shadows harbour

mysterious inlets which you – like a moth – will wish to avoid by keeping to the light. Tonight, light – more than I – will be your guide.

I relieve you of your umbrella and newspaper, for this is the hall: the place between the out-of-doors and in. It is here where I, your host, meet you and where you will receive an invitation to proceed further. Its position half-way between the outside and in gave birth to an image of halls containing things needed for that transition: boots, raincoats, hats, guns. Originally any large house was a 'hall': one room built around a central hearth for communal habitation. Only later, for privacy's sake, were side-hearths – or fireplaces – developed, which were then partitioned off to create the room. Thus a house is a collection of rooms under one roof, with its hall serving both the front door and its more private parts within. Its historic origins might make us imagine it furnished with antiquated relics such as sets of dusty antlers, stuffed animal heads, suits of armour and weaponry, as well as – always – some primitive old timepiece. Chairs were not upholstered – for who knows what strangers from outside might carry in with them?

20

As was common in the early eighteenth century, the house was originally purchased as a brick shell, and a joiner was then commissioned to assemble rooms with partitioning – or panels – constructed of pine, or deal. You stand, therefore, inside a piece of furniture with each room like a drawer within a chest of drawers, and each with its own quirky characteristics and features. Like the interior of an old ship, there is a wooden tightness, and its creakiness reminds us that it is its business to protect and embrace. A door slams shut upstairs.

Ah . . . and there it is; tossed over the newel post of the stairs is the merchant's jacket, wig and tricorne hat. He may have just dashed away and out of sight, but how strong his presence is: stronger than anything visible in wood, metal or plaster. I watch your eyes dart to a piece of paper pinned to the silk, but instead of finding a description or a label as you might in a museum, you find its owner's name: a French name, Mr Isaac Gervais.

Now, perhaps because of an illustration in a children's book or an old painting, or maybe an advertisement for pipe tobacco or chocolate, something might make you see this man dressed, as Georgian gentlemen were, in three parts. Shoes and hose to the knees; then breeches, waistcoat and skirted jacket, topped with a wig and tricorne hat.

Believe me . . .
This house, and
your adventure
within it, is
all about three

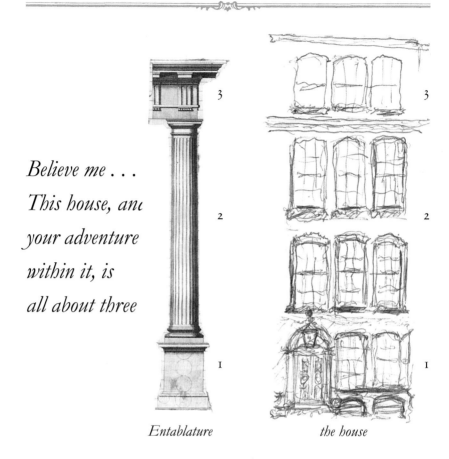

Entablature   the house

'*All about three,*' I say, startling you with a voice and a stare. At the same time I gesture away from myself and behind me to both sides. '*See? Everything around you; the wall's panelling, the long-cased clock, the hall chair and tripod table — the exterior of this or any other eighteenth-century town house . . . are all pieced together to be seen in three parts.*'

Some instinct asks us to size things up, whether it be a meal or a discussion, in three parts: a beginning, a middle and an end. For our own survival something tells us to lift ourselves up above the ground to the dry safety of a base on which we can work and live. High overhead, on a shelf — so to speak, and at a safe distance from the

*section of hall
panelling*

the clock

*and therefore –
the man*

dangers of the ground and the turmoil created by our toil – we keep our best things/possessions: our art. In architecture and design this is represented by the *pedestal* (base), the *column* and the *capital*.

Your eyes have now adjusted from the outside light to this new one indoors, from daylight to candlelight; from your own time to another: one which, though it may be new to you, the house insists is *Now*.

I gesture to you to follow me down the ten wooden steps under the main staircase to the basement room below. No longer the reader; with some hesitation you are now inside. Now you are my visitor.

CHAPTER THREE

THE ONLY PLACE TO BEGIN

Within, the colour *black* is the only place to begin. You might remember from your childhood that things are easier to imagine in the dark. ¶ With ten steps down and the door behind us closed, we just catch sight of the last morsel of evening light filtering down through the cellar's only window; it is patched together with dirty, cracked and broken leaded lights; grown over by moss and fern on the outside and festooned within by cobwebs laden with damp dust. Barely visible is this damp, dark basement area, with a ceiling so low that it brushes the tops of our heads, and a floor so broken by time and wear that it has almost returned to the ground. Under the window is what seems to be some sort of abandoned excavation. It is all you can really see; for any second now the colour black will have its way, and begin its nightly reign. Only then will we begin to see . . . in the dark.

I light the single candle which I passed through the frame to reveal the cellar, or 'back kitchen', used for the storage of fuel, wine and kitchen supplies. Visitors sit here amid stacks of dusty bottles, piles of logs and soiled laundry, so they will sense that there is always life somewhere nearby.

You stare at me nervously, as if asking for instructions, and in turn I reply by asking you to be seated, saying as I do, *'Your seat, I am afraid, is very low to the ground.'* A set of ancient hearth chairs is arranged in a half-circle to face the excavation under the window. The chairs were purposely constructed to sit low so that in those primitive hovels with a central fire, and no chimney, the occupants could sit as close to the fire's warmth as possible while still remaining under the cloud of smoke which drifted above them seeking an escape. To this I add, *'A memory of the discomforts of being so low to the ground is essential to man's first step towards sophistication. We start . . . from here.'*

The empty chairs on either side of you are normally taken by the seven other guests who participate in what happens. However, unknown to you, tonight the visitor is you alone.

The stones of the abandoned excavation before us are a small part of the remains of the twelfth-century lepers' hospice, St Mary's Spital. As your eyes move to it, so your ears hear the oddest thing, one that in these circumstances must feel ominous: the sound of a human heartbeat.

Boom-boom, boom-boom, boom-boom . . . and here, so near to the birthplace of Mr Sweeney Todd, within the haunts of the legendary

26

Jack the Ripper, I assure you of something I can see you are pleased to hear: that I do not murder and then bury my victims here in this cellar. No. The excavation before us was begun by the Gervais children in the late eighteenth century when they suddenly developed a curiosity for the past. It was continued by the children of successive generations as a rainy-day amusement until tools were downed in 1897 on the eve of Queen Victoria's Diamond Jubilee, when the house became the setting for a large family gathering. *'Oddly enough,'* I say aloud, but almost to myself, *'seven hundred years – to the very year – after the Priory's founding in 1197.'*

'Look!... This is not only medieval. The children must have also discovered and imagined Romans, Normans, Elizabethans, Stuarts and Georgians too – all from the soil of this crater.' Baffled, you ponder.

I blow out the flame in the instant that the door springs open to send a shaft of lamplight sweeping across the crude brick floor to land directly at your feet. Like the moth, our route is again decided by instinct, to glide toward that light and to the warmth and comfort it suggests. And with no alternative other than damp and dark, I sense your relief as we do.

CHAPTER FOUR

'HOME'

Through a picture frame we re-emerge into what could be the hovel lodged between the roots of a tree in a children's story. A domestic dream, with a low crooked ceiling and large dresser with colourful crockery stacked to its full height; a table of scrubbed pine covered with wooden bowls and baskets, all spilling over with green vegetables, white turnips, brown onions and bright orange carrots. This is undoubtedly the house's kitchen and the smell of freshly baked pastry, the light of candles and the warmth radiating from the fire that burns so merrily in an old kitchen range, all tell us so. Here black is warmed from the inside out to blossom into honey. Pure poetry: if this picture has a label, then it must be 'Home'.

And what a difference! Although the room is the same size and shape as the cellar next to it, the sensation it gives is the perfect opposite: light and warmth. Cold and dark haven't got a chance. Yes – low in the basement and under a very low ceiling, but with the candlelight reflecting off the glazes on old teacups and crockery, off polished brass and copper pots and pans, and with the red flames licking round the hissing black kettle – warmth and light have won. A moment of silence reveals that the heartbeat which set the pulse of Time next door is here turned into the real tick-tock of an old wall clock. And what's this? . . . hello! The room's cat has jumped up on to the table and is lifting her tail and trumping out loud miaows to salute our arrival. Here in a basement in the centre of Europe's largest city, we seem to have come across a little paradise: a domestic Garden of Eden.

31

Refuge

My definition of a home changes from time to time, but in recent years, it has come to mean refuge.

Buying my own house made me begin to reflect and ask myself just what – in my own mind – I wanted 'home' to be. Coming from an affluent part of southern California during the great boom of the Sixties this was sometimes confusing, for I was continually aware of a phenomenon I saw as *Everything and Nothing*. Those with a talent for making money tended to spend it on mountains of material things that distanced them more and more from what they, and their homes, really were. It made them abandon their own originality to take on something aspired to as 'style'. Swimming pools and two-car garages spoke, and were listened to, with reverence.

All this conflicted with 'home' – as I knew it, for home to me was certainly never anything remotely material. It consisted, I have decided, in something I sensed as refuge: an atmosphere of safety in the love between my parents. It came in a tone of voice, in the preparation and the eating of meals, in conversations during washing up and being busy in the garden. It went with us when we travelled. I am always slightly perplexed when I hear people speak of home as being 'country', 'Art Deco', 'Late Georgian' or 'circa 1540'; for in my own case home was nothing, but it had everything. What I dreaded most was a statement I heard someone make as they emerged from a wealthy household devised to impress, *'No joy . . . of purchase or possession.'* One Australian journalist – writing for a Sydney arts page – opened his eyes to gesture around him at the contents of this house and ask, *'How many? . . . ever counted them all?'*

One bookend of my home was lost when I was eleven and my mother died after a long illness. My father and I watched the idea of home go into reverse, and I can remember my own insecurity when he took me by the hand to say, *'I think maybe it's time to go back to the house now.'* In this reverse way I began to know what others meant by 'home'.

At the age of sixteen I wanted the whole of England to be my home, and was quite happy to hitch-hike about a nation of dream houses while bedding down outside them at nights on park benches and barns, in bus shelters and – more to my liking – in church porches. In those days gaol cells often sat empty and policemen had bigger hearts, and on two occasions I had one assigned to me as my night's lodgings. It was when I was a homeless student traveller that one night I heard *hearth* and *home* used as the same word. It immediately struck a chord.

As I huddled before the open fires that blazed away in market places in those days, I began to notice that an atmosphere of fellowship and refuge would develop among strangers, even if none in the circle spoke. I looked through window panes at a nation on the brink of abandoning coal fires as the heart of their homes to see the last stage of a long evolution: little circles of society protected within little boxes.

People often ask how someone who claims that the late twentieth century is a little too old-fashioned for his liking can have no desire for its electrical gadgetry or modern heating. The answer is, quite simply, taste. Any shortage will draw closer together what little there is and turn it into quality. Good restaurants are not overlit, nor are they too warm, nor will they serve you so much food that facing it becomes a chore. Too much light, heat or comfort breeds a self-containment that kills the natural nucleus in the dynamics of a home. In this house even my relationship with my cat is more closely drawn in. And for sure, from the very instant the chimney huffed, puffed and heaved to draw smoke once more, I watched this room pull together – cat and all – to begin a life of its own.

Later on, when I was a student, two very special and quite different families made their large country houses feel like home to me, and while I stored what I collected in their attics and stable buildings, the life in these households made an undying impression. I stood back to analyse their charm with almost scientific scrutiny. I needed to establish in my mind what I would ideally, one day, like for myself. However, I could see that more than any commodity, a good home was only as good as its family. Looking back, it has only recently occurred to me that what impressed me also cost . . . money.

It was when I came to London as a student that I found the visual ideal which was to impress me most; a room seen through a window in the Furniture Department of the Victoria and Albert Museum. At least once a week I left my student squalor to gawk through a plate glass window at a museum display, 'a room of the early Georgian period'.

I didn't have to be told, as I was continually, that this was only a display and lacked life; I loved the look of it and it continued to inspire me to collect things. At one stage, with starvation and collecting both well on their way, I began to get a little anxious. Could the cynics be right? Maybe you *can't* live in a place that looks like another time? Maybe my heart and lungs *will* seize up if what surrounds me doesn't come from Harrods, Peter Jones or Tottenham Court Road. However, another more practical peek through that same window revealed chairs to sit on, tables to eat at, carpets to stand on, a fireplace for warmth and candlesticks for light. And also, with a quick glance in the opposite direction at the horrors of modern shops, I decided that yes, of course I am going to live *in there* – even if I get arrested for it. I will build myself a museum

display and kick its door open; build a fire and cook in it, eat in it, sleep, pee in it, and like it or not, give it life.

On 12 August 1979, instead of kicking it down I collected a key and unlocked the door of 18 Folgate Street to do just that. My solicitor, with me at the time, had some surprising news: that the sitting tenant – with whom I had expected to share the house – had died since I signed the contract. All five floors and ten rooms were suddenly mine.

So too was the street – mine. With no neighbours I was at liberty to do whatever I wanted, and for the first time since I arrived in England, I was able to let loose and be creative without anyone nearby saying or implying: '*Surely – you can't do that . . .*', though a few did try.

It was to be one room at a time, finished to perfection, and my first efforts were concentrated here in the kitchen: for eating is both instinctive and hereditary. Though much of the ceiling was lying under my feet on the floor and the carcass of a dead dog had been tossed down through a broken window from the street, the fabric of the room was complete. The original dresser and wooden interior were here, the sash windows with thick glazing bars, the fireplace and even the original lead plumbing and linseed white paint, all honey-brown with age. All very exciting, all still intact. The objects I had collected over the years were washed, cleaned and set nicely in

position. As I put them in there, I found myself turning more and more to the one thing that people commented on most. Atmosphere: the *space between* things.

Atmosphere is free and I couldn't afford to ask for grants; as a foreigner in a host country, and as someone too independent to believe in 'benefits', I hadn't a bean. I found plenty to eat abandoned in the market each morning, which I would then boil up over a fire made from the broken wooden pallets also left behind there. Yes, atmosphere is free, so on it I would have to feed. With not a penny available for rewiring, and with the old electricity cables rotted away on the basement floor, the first thing I did was to light the fire in the kitchen hearth and begin to build my new life from there.

While I worked, friends would often turn up and I sensed their enjoyment of what was, I guess, a real-life urban adventure. I was

Mickey Rooney-in-the-East. They revelled in all the chaos for which I was so busy apologising. This made me look back and recall how exciting it was to arrive at a house and be rushed aside by a member of the family, who would then inform me that something delicate was going on in the background. I decided that I liked houses with lives of their own, which you were expected to catch hold of and ride with – like a cruise or a carousel. What this house needed, I was the first to admit, was a family.

Out of Sight

I found a family abandoned in the streets and alleys of the East End – loudspeakers, which I looted from the backs of discarded television sets. I then recorded domestic sounds: voices, crying babies, bottles being uncorked with glasses being filled, collected and washed; fires poked and clocks wound – all recorded here within the house's own wooden acoustics. Then I placed the speakers under the floorboards and inside the cupboards, for this family was destined – like the real source of sound anywhere – to remain out of sight.

However, soon I began to see that the people I'd created were something of a responsibility. Callers and 'friends' would turn up who would insist that the family conform correctly to the discipline prescribed by the early eighteenth-century Huguenot merchant tradition here in Spitalfields. I realised that I would have to protect them and prevent them from getting involved in 'real' history, and keep them from ever being seduced by the Class Hoax. I chose the most *nobody* name I could think of: Gervais – later to be spelled Jervis, which no one interesting enough to get cornered by fame could ever conceivably want to have and keep without having to wear tweeds to compensate for it.

To balance the fiction, the next step for my family was to ensure that whatever actually stands before the eye should be as *real as real can be*: a larger-than-life state of practical reality. Here in the kitchen this would of course have to be in the preparation, cooking and transportation of food. To this should be added a smell and a certain sort of wear and tear, a chore abandoned in mid-process, or even a half-eaten dish of cat food – all these led to the development of the house's own art form, 'life interrupted' or the 'Still Life Drama'.

Baby-sitting

'*. . . nothing to explain,*' I say looking around me to suggest the magic formula. '*To everything you see, form and function are one – a pitcher from which to pour, a plate from which to eat . . . any question as to what or why is smothered at birth by its own answer.*'

Sure enough, there is nothing to explain: no pretensions and no disappointments. There are certainly no 'antiques' in little display cases, and no single object will dare step forward to steal the limelight from the whole effect by making itself the star. All the objects here have come together to cradle something, or someone, they all share – *between*.

The room's spell is thus described as 'Man before the Fall'. You see home is a refuge in which you – as when still in your mother's arms – don't have to think or feel to stay alive. Your innocence is safe, warm, protected; you give yourself to it and its heartbeat: in this room you may simply be.

. . . what's that?

As you sit before the fire with the cat on one knee, I watch and wait for the right time to say, *'What was that sound?'* Then: *'. . . the candles: are they not flickering more than before? Is something . . . teasing them?'* You blink twice before seeing out into the air as I turn round to look behind me. The cat is awakened by a tension she intercepts through your knee: you are drawing away from your soul to revert to using your mind; to think.

After taking a slow, cool look around, you turn to me with an expression that announces suspicion of some kind of conspiracy. I too respond by looking away and from place to place – but manage to catch and hold your eye. I sniff into the air as it fills with the smell of cooking. A distant voice: whose? Confused, you watch hard as I focus and then suddenly freeze. *'Rebecca Philpot.'* I turn to you and my eyes widen as I gesture at the large, bulbous, bentwood carver chair which sits between us beside the fire. I add, *'Four feet five inches tall, with bright red hair and blue eyes. Her motto: "Never mind your own business."'*

Again I direct your gaze to a cream jug sitting on the dresser – full-blown, bulbous and flowery; now to the fire and to the hissing kettle, also bulbous. All different and yet somehow related; through a common outline.

Am I suggesting what you think I am? That the mob cap, the apron, all those jugs, the kettle and the jars – are all, in this flickering candlelight, supposed to join together to construct someone generic, of a certain bulbous likeness and type that would fit snugly into that chair? That, as with one of those old-time character actors in black and white films, we are to visualise a type already lodged in our subconscious which everything around us here is inviting to come out? I am indeed.

Rebecca Philpot. Some may know her as the 'pot that calls the tea kettle black', who can sometimes behave like 'a herring on a griddle', who has 'gone to pot', who is seen each night tightening the ropes of her mattress in order to 'sleep tight'. She picks up the kind of stories that travel (badly) between the Cock and the Bull public houses in Farringdon, and preserves the chewy bit of bone – the 'paddywack' – from the neck of mutton – so as to 'give a dog a bone'.

Her moral leanings are brutally symmetrical: from the soul – 'an eye for an eye – a tooth for a tooth'. The children are sent up the stairs with 'a candle to light them to bed'; and with the balanced alternative of 'a chopper, to chop off their heads'. Poor Rebecca; found here at the end of each day adjusting the knotted ropes of her own mattress in her never-ceasing quest to 'sleep tight'.

'Rock-a-bye-baby . . .' and my eyes lead yours to the corner of the table, where a child's highchair is grouped with a miniature cup and saucer filled with tea, a half-eaten carrot and a number of toys. Rebecca has been baby-sitting. Apparently she keeps the sleepy child

contented by employing 'nursery rhymes', rhymes that rock to the symmetry of her own heartbeat – as well as to the tick-tock of the room's clock. Rock-a-bye-baby . . . and so, at least in this room, do I.

'*Will you look at her?*' I say, turning again to Rebecca's chair and shaking my head with a look of playful – if soured – resignation. '*In repose; uncompromisingly solid. No saint, she – carrying about a full-blown opinion of herself – always speaking in "triumphs". You should know that cooking and general housekeeping are combined with a full programme of other activities, including scheming, mischief-making, gossiping and the artful fabrication of self-advancing lies. Like a half-hidden stream are underlying themes of superstition, low prejudice, and religious bigotry. And yet*', and my voice makes a curious change as we both stare at the same chair anew, '*she does have an exceedingly large, round soul.*' And I perk up to ask, '*Don't you think?*'

True. You gaze at the chair and again almost smile. For sure, this particular bentwood carver chair is almost round in construction, as

if it was the work of a cooper, and would draw you in and close its
eyes if it were to hug you to its lap.

Rebecca Philpot comes and goes, but
disappears into the kitchen's not-so-thin air
whenever a visitor begins to name or count the
ordinary crocks and utensils which other
visitors like to picture her using. That, or when
someone tries to work out her age in numbers.
It might be a pleasant thing to hold in her
memory that when one smiled at Rebecca
Philpot, she would stick the tip of her tongue
into her left cheek first and *then* smile back.

Now – hidden beneath a white linen cover is something too
complicated for so simple a place; it might wake us into asking the
kind of questions that would ruin our new-found contentment.
Seeing you move in its direction, I warn, *'It might be planted there as a
temptation – like the forbidden fruit in the Garden of Eden . . . to separate us
from our soul.'* Most visitors decide to lift the cover; it's either that or
they begin to open my cupboards and drawers.

Lifted, it is a cone of sparkling white
granules. Unlike anything else in the room it
does indeed stand out. Heaving a sigh, I explain,
*'In both colour and shape it is quite unfamiliar; foreign,
it is a "sugar loaf".'* All this is said in the
appropriate affected staccato voice of a trained
museum interpreter. I now begin to crank-start
your mental intelligence.

*'Sugar was transported in this form to England
from the West Indies. Americans ask for "cubes", we in
England still ask for "lumps" of sugar – from the*

practice of snipping pieces off the loaf with "sugar crushers" and taking them to the rooms where they were needed to sweeten drinks. The early Europeans in Rio de Janeiro were sugar traders and they named the great volcanic mount that greeted them after their loaves of sugar . . .'

And so our minds could go on – and on and on – until everything on our planet is seen as related through a sugar loaf. Now that your mind is in charge, you can no longer *be*, but will begin picking through the contents of this room. You could turn my kitchen into a museum display called: 'A typical room of the eighteenth century'.

The Real World Awakes!

'Listen! . . . upstairs? Listen!' In the distance a baby is heard crying while a bell mounted up on one wall behind us begins to spring back and forth to summon a certain servant. *'Hear it?'* I say turning to you accusingly. *'You have set the real world into motion.'* I toss a wax candle end on to the fire to make the flames climb and the range spit. In the room above us chairs are being pulled back, footsteps scuff, gruff voices – people above us are beginning to move round in circles. Who's up there?

Time to stop *being*; Time to start *thinking*. Out of a frying pan and into a fire.

Open-up . . .

Private

PART TWO

Back and Forth
— This House
and Your Mind

CHAPTER FIVE

ADOLESCENCE

You see, leaving the nest for the real world means that there is no other choice but to use your two legs and walk; two feet, two legs, two hands – survival is all about *two*. We start clumsily; co-ordination takes experience, practice and Time. ¶ At a certain age all those nursery rhymes, stories – religious or otherwise, along with the playthings and fantasies which formerly eased our consciousness into various states of contentment – are suddenly no longer *real* enough. Life interrupts, and exposure to the world provides the pressure to make us sharpen up and focus on things directly. Compound intelligence is thus born. To be smart, no fancy must get in the way of what our mind's eye can plainly see. Our success at physical and mental co-ordination depends on a lack of any slack between our self and what we see. To admit to seeing the invisible – the space between – is, to the gang, at least, weird, infantile or retarded.

So now it becomes *Them versus Us: our* own family, gang, class, school or race; our own type versus an enemy who is not our type: when we are insecure and nervous, strength lies in numbers. And even if – in the kitchen – a little girl might turn a twig into a doll and a little boy the same twig into a gun, a separation will soon become natural. So it's boys or girls; the traitors who get too close to the border are 'tomboys' or 'sissies'.

So here we go. Back in the hall, I stand you before a pair of double doors and ask you to close your eyes. At first you resist, but now I insist. *'You must close your eyes to help you to see.'* Outside – and coming nearer – is the clippity-clop, clippity-clop, louder and louder of horses' hooves. A horseman rides up and past the door and then softer and softer – softer and softer – he rides on by. I whisper: *'Where? . . . when . . . are we?'*

I ask you to open your eyes slowly and concentrate on the thick black paint on the back of the doors. After a pause I say, *'Apply your hands to both sides of the door; crack them open at the centre, and then gently, very gently, push back both sides.'*

At first – only the sparkle and twinkle of a few candles. Then, and all the time still unfolding, the doors spread further apart to expose the very scene you imagined above you while down in the kitchen. Yes, there it is. And more stunning too than I think you could ever imagine. A baroque painting, in three dimensions, its sitters – you remember – have only just walked away and out of sight.

A table surrounded by a circle of abandoned high-back chairs, all of which are pointing inwards in the direction of a full-blown still-life drama. A cascade of fruit, towered over by a tall toasting  glass and a candlestick, spills at us from a chipped delft dish. Other glasses too, some with air-twist stems, spiral upwards to support bowls still marked with finger-prints and filled with the dregs of sweet red wine. Green grapes, red plums, apples and pears, each with baroque contours twinkle with speckles of dew drops as an insect with red and orange wings crawls up and over a plum to disappear again. Blue and white dishes and buff-grey pewter stand side by side, competing with the richer reflection of polished silver and a solid gold wedding ring. Crumpled white linen napkins lie on the table, crushed crumbs are still underfoot, and the aroma of rosemary and roast lamb rushes at us in the draught of the room's escaping warmth. You stand before it . . . stupefied. Good.

'*Rich, eh?*' Issued with a nod, I float a caption so that it rides within the draught. *'Just imagine it . . . all around us outside – London; full of the tales of Moll Flanders and Robinson Crusoe. Highwayman Dick Turpin has begun his famous "ride" from just up the road at Aldgate – to York. Halley has spied his comet; George I is gravely ill; Sir Isaac Newton and Sir Christopher Wren have only just died.*' To which I add in a very certain tone, '*But the house is brand new, and so too, for you, is this World in Time.*'

As you focus in silence and stare ahead, *clippity-clop, clippity-clop, clippity-clop*, and then on by.

Clink-Clank

Clink, clank, goes the crude mechanism of the room's old brass clock. I ask if you've ever noticed how newly-weds often want to start out life with everything matching. Well – so did the baroques, and what a meal they made of it. They saw themselves as *above and apart* from Nature, as the 'crown of creation'. They took their cue on how to co-ordinate things from the symmetry of their own human form. So will we. To do so advertised that they could stand on their own two feet: that they were 'together', and therefore in control. Pairs of candlesticks, pairs of chairs, pairs of pier glasses, consoles and even pairs of dolls. (Do visit Lord and Lady Clapham in the Victoria and Albert Museum.) Wigs had centre partings; patches (beauty marks) were worn on one side of the face by 'Tories' – and on the other side by 'Whigs'. Children lined up to enter the school gates flanked by charming painted figures of *Boy* and *Girl*, while lunatics were carted into Bedlam Hospital through gates flanked by a pair of huge carved figures representing the two directions of madness: *melancholia* and *mania*. Both sides laughed at [♂] puppet – '*Punch*' – on one side, beating other puppet [♀] – '*Judy*' – over the head with a club. Music was being separated into two parts to make it counterpoint. Architecture too was balanced, as we know from the famous view of Greenwich Palace from the river, or of the Royal Hospital at Chelsea with two highly defined sides pushed together to stand and pose as one. All as uncomfortably formal as a traditional wedding photograph.

Like Noah's Ark, this room is all about *two*, but is not intended to stand as the ideal couple, but more like a pair of late sovereigns, still near to our time, King William of Orange and Queen Mary II. Imagine them together: he short, military, asthmatic and Dutch; she

Clink . . . clank . . .

Puritan – OR – Cavalier

"Whig" – OR – "Tory"

King Louis XIV – OR – William of Orange

OR

King George! – – King James!

". . . Too Little" OR "Too Much"

Catholic – OR – Protestant

A Palace at Versailles? – OR – one at Hampton Court?

North – OR – South

Free-Thinking – OR – "The Old Faith"

"Too wide" Like brown bread or white: it's all "Too wide"

Man – OR – Woman

Either one The other

"Punch – OR – "Judy"

Man Woman

Culture OR Nature

Black – OR – White

Scottish, one foot taller, porcelain complexioned and serene. Nevertheless, they were pushed by politics and war to stand together and hold their two States as one. This room looks like the way it sounds, with the clink-clank of its old brass clock. There is no bonding honey-coloured soul flowing between any two things here: it's red and white, blue and white, green and white, black and white, clink, clank, one against the other; bold.

The room's mission is one of dualism. The sharp and colourful contrasts divide your perception, waking you up to the fact that anything we may know about the baroque is usually only a single leg of this two-legged energy. There were two sides of the same spell in force, in balance or opposition, just as there are still in Northern Ireland today. On bad days they flexed, hated and warred, on good days, like William and Mary, they stood awkwardly alongside one another.

'Listen to the old brass clock . . . Clink . . . clank. Clank . . . clank . . .'

I gesture at the still life before us, and within it a pewter jug and a tall toasting glass. The tall glass contains a toast to the Protestant Cause, while the jug is kept empty. I explain that Isaac, a Protestant, is attempting to trap any clandestine Catholic Jacobite who might pass his glass over water to toast the 'King over the water' – James II – in exile in France, instead of that of the Protestant George of Hanover. Even today, only the queen herself is trusted with a fingerbowl of water at a state banquet. The word limp comes into the English language from a toast to 'L' for Louis XIV, 'I' for James II, 'M' for Mary of Modena (his wife), and 'P' for the Prince of Wales (the 'Bonnie Prince'). That loyalty can be, to Isaac Gervais, only to one side. If someone is *limp*, he or she is cursed with a weakness and vulnerability to the other, opposing, side.

None of this would have happened in the kitchen, for down

'. . . limp?

It's a trap; don't get caught.'

there the good soul we saw at work before the fire would simply abide with and tend to whatever came her way. It would warn our minds that actions based on such things constitute a sin; and that the word kindness means to treat all of our species as we would our own kind.

'*It is the year 1727; two sides to everything – which is yours?*' Still standing behind, I often feel terror shoot through the visitor as I ask emphatically. '*Limp? Clink or clank, you really must decide. Everyone else has.*' You look across the empty room – as if you suddenly suspect that someone might be hiding in one of its corners.

I whisper, '*Do you believe that your own life is decided by Divine Providence? That is, by* God? or: *Do you believe in* Free Will? *That is, that God gave you what you need to decide and negotiate your destiny – for yourself?*'

This I continue with, '*You know the expression. "It all boils down to . . .?" Well, all this – even the friction between England and America, nature or nurture – it all boils down to this same argument: do we use initiative in the face of God? Or, do we hold back – use our powers of restraint – in the face of God?'*

Now in one ear I whisper: *'You know . . . "Sow nothing, reap nothing": sit back and do nothing and what can you expect?'* Then in the other ear, *'On the contrary! If we had left things alone in the first place – then the problem would have never arisen.'*

All about two: the terms *Catholic* (universal) and *Protestant* (protest-ant) imply conflict: any case made in favour of the one will invariably become an insult to the other. It is, however, a conflict that exists inside us all, and floats *between* our two natural leanings: *meant to be* – or Divine Providence – and to *take control* – Free Will. It is the inside story of every hour of every day of all our lives.

A room to get your back up

Oh! – and to have the chance to point out that the chairs are too old for the supposed date of the room; that the colour on the walls is 'wrong', and that the portrait over the fire is of George III, who didn't come to the throne until 1760. Given half a chance the same spirit of 'honesty' might also make you take a blowtorch to the paint to expose a knot-hole in the panelling; maybe even to pickle and then wax it. However, as adolescent or nouveau-intellectual as this may seem to me, it makes a visitor walk right-smack-dab into the room's plot.

To get your back up more I should explain that – to me – 'art' is beauty in balance. And if you can't rise above the street business of identifying things when both are combined before you, then 'art' is not your level. Tonight, pigeonhole intelligence is not going to win by ruining the pictures I paint in the space between us. You will not

64

return what I create in your mind by reducing it to a palette of paint with a name and number for each ingredient. And besides, I suspect that I can ask your questions for you, *'But, aren't you frightened of fire?'* *'Who does all the cleaning?'* *'You can't actually live here?'* *'Where do you hide your microwave?'* (Ha, ha!) *'Did they really paint their rooms such dark colours?'* *'I'm cold; I'm hot . . . I couldn't exist without a hair drier.'* *'But don't you realise that people actually died back in those days?'* No, not tonight and not here: no questions. The house motto is, *'You either see it or you don't.'*

However, one question is a step in the right direction: one that separates Man from Nature: *'Did they really sit in those uncomfortably stiff-looking, high-backed chairs?'* The house's late-baroque inhabitants had only to look out of these windows at those who lived on the streets to realise that what saved them from the same fate was their ability to lift themselves above danger. As you will remember from the cellar, the poor huddled to the ground and sat low. The Baroques are using their wits to tighten up and discipline themselves for the sake of survival; so that they rule their lives as opposed to allowing their lives to rule them. So upright a chair advertises just such a baroque aspiration. And yes, I believe that you too might wish to sit in such a high, stiff and bone-upright chair; especially if you think I am watching you, and that those like yourself are all doing the same?

However, something about this room will remind you that it was only one side of the baroque that wished to appear as if it had risen so high above Nature that it could become the god-like figures carved in marble who never had to work. That side did indeed wear waistcoats and skirted jackets of embroidered and flowered silks, with big buttons, big sleeves – all trimmed with silver and gold lustrings. Big, big, big . . . but doing so would not be above us either; if fashion and economics favoured the display of success and wealth. The other side to all this is the response you may feel at the mention of dirt, head lice or fleas: to *purify* things by making things clean and simple: to become a 'Puritan'. Both sides are stored within.

I say, *'We have only to travel in Time to find that one part of us or the other, has already got there and made itself the better part of an Age – look at "New Labour".'* And after catching your attention – I whisper across the table. *'Clink-clank, and which are you?'* Looking both ways: *'Be careful . . . not to get found out.'*

Mr Isaac Gervais,
of Folgate Street, Spitalfields

CHAPTER SIX

A VERY LOP-SIDED CONFECTION

'. . . *and here, seated before us, is the Protestant himself: Mr Isaac Gervais.*' So I say, stepping forward to halt before one of the chairs standing at the table. With the surprising strength of the room's atmosphere, and with its floor being at such a slant, it is hard to think straight. ¶ Thus I introduce the aura in the *space between* that chair and your eyes as Mr Isaac Gervais. ¶ Now, to be a boringly authentic Protestant room, free of any fancy deceptions and with nothing to hide, the room should be painted a clean, simple white. We are however, encased in walls painted a dark (gloss) olive green; so strong that the candlelight will reflect a variant of that

colour into the air of the room. In this colour you now stand, and in the alcove on your left is a portrait of Isaac Gervais set against a background of the same colour. He sits in it, we stand in it, but we all breathe an air of the same colour. What lingers directly before us here in a pool of warmth is a small mass of late-baroque energy which I am now about to mask with a face and figure.

Isaac's wig still hangs where gentlemen tend to hang them once their womenfolk are sent away; over one of the two finials of the chair's high back. *'A very upright man,'* I say, checking you first before looking at him with a nod. I bring him more into sight: your eyes wander to his wine glass filled with dregs and marked with fingerprints to suggest how it was held; to the bite taken out of his apple, not yet brown. Now to a letter which bears his name, and to a long clay pipe half-packed with newly chopped tobacco, with a twist of old book-leaf paper to light it. Plenty for the imagination to do *between*, without merely assigning the names and dates to things on the perimeter.

A pedestal, column and capital – and so too we see him dressed. Shoes and hose, waistcoat and jacket, wig and tricorne. We might fill out his figure a little further with the shape of the decanter on the table (a *crucible* bottle). For it certainly suggests the popular outline of the gentlemen's jackets, with their narrow tailored shoulders and stiffly boned skirts, just as it echoes the ladies' outline: wide from the front and narrow from the side, the panniers of the day. The rest of Mr Gervais's apparel, his shoes, stock and wig, will all determine his poise and movement. The tie of the stock around his neck, of course, determines the pitch of his cough.

'*To see him otherwise . . .*', I tell you with a suggestion of a twinkle, '*would take an almost unnatural degree of imagination.*'

'*Isaac Gervais's family . . .*', I lean closer to say, while turning once more to check the double doors behind me, '*like many thousands of Huguenot families, were slaughtered in France on the order of the Catholic Louis XIV in or around the year 1685. He himself, orphaned, was smuggled out of France by a faithful nurse and carried to England's protecting shore concealed in a wine cask.*'

The Holy Bible in the room reminds us that the printing press brought the Reformation and men like Isaac Gervais into being. He learned to read and write so that he would not have to lean on or trust anyone else with their interpretation of *the word.* He is therefore independent. This, and the Puritan work ethic – pleasing God by way of his work – opened the world up for him as it had for other Protestants. It contributed to making Mr Gervais successful and a wealthy master silk weaver of Spitalfields.

He reads into his Protestantism not only his own independence, but also a fresh sense of new liberty from an old world held back by darkness and superstition. He would no more say 'Good Luck' or 'Good Fortune' than he would play cards, place bets on horses, or partake in games of chance. '*Why?*' – he would ask an Irish Roman Catholic priest holding a racing card. Such things are uncertain and cannot be calculated to pay real dividends. This more scientific approach to life soon developed into the markets for stocks and shares, insurance and assurance, with the world centre for insurance up the road from here in London at Lloyd's coffee house.

Isaac does do lots of things, secretly however, and he is known to play about a bit by letting his mind wander off into one of those bawdy new *novels* (meaning new), which have been getting more and more popular. Like the ones written by Henry Fielding a few years later in which the imagination is taken off the rational track by fiction and philosophical discourses. His faith in the good mind that God gave him will then bring him back, whereas once – or so it was supposed by the Church – it might not.

'*For, after all,*' so I turn and ask, '*is a novel not really only just a dolled-up lie?*' I often wonder if my visitors realise that what we are doing here tonight is itself very Protestant. If someone from the regime of the Old Faith a century before Isaac's time had walked through this door to find us conjuring up such things, we might all be dragged off to Smithfield and burned at the stake for heresy.

Free Will makes Old Isaac see his life as a form of professional journey, or *career*. Like the present-day American celebration of Hallowe'en – as opposed to the strict and serious Old World observance of All Souls' Day – he makes a mockery of such things as are spiritually mysterious. He burns a big dummy of the conspirator *Guy* Fawkes, and makes plenty of noise as a warning to the Other Side on the fifth of November. Instead of Mardi Gras or Carnival to take him into Lent, Mr Gervais would turn the Shrove Tuesday before Ash Wednesday into something practical by allowing his wife to splurge at wasting the last of the season's flour on pancakes instead of bread.

Gesturing at the table, I remind you that most forms of conventional patriotism are left over from the side of us, and in particular the response to the campaign to defend the Protestant Cause from the supposed threat of the alternative led by Bonnie Prince Charlie in the Jacobite rebellion of 1745, 'The 45'. The prince, backed by Roman Catholic France and Spain, set Spitalfields in a frenzy when he began to march his troops south from Scotland. Above us Mr Gervais's sword rests across the portrait of the latest imported Protestant sovereigns, at the ready. Isaac sees the first two Georges as 'Warriors of the Cause', and George I as a hero, the last British king personally to lead his troops into battle. flags and royal coats of arms were hung in churches; songs like 'Rule Britannia!' were written, loyal toasts were drunk and church bells rung.

He is sure that his son knows that the pope himself was responsible for the Great fire of London of 1666; and in 1745 he contributed to the expense of having this piece of invented history added to the inscription on the stone base of the Monument, by Sir Christopher Wren, in the City. He insists that Rebecca should rock young Edward to sleep with the glad news of Protestant William of Orange's arrival in England: '*Rock-a-bye baby* (hiding) *in the* (orange) *tree top, when the* (Protestant wind) *blows, the cradle* (Catholic throne) *will rock. When the bow* (of his ship) *breaks* (anchors), *baby* (Roman Catholic – James II) *will fall, then down will come baby, cradle* (Roman Catholic – throne, crown, court) *and all!*'

Man OR Woman

'*Well, . . . what is there to like?*' I once heard a woman remark as she watched Isaac leaving the French Chapel in Church Street. '*Are we to fall on our knees before the wealth he has amassed for himself? He wants to be respected, well fine! But liking him is quite another matter; one for which there is little on offer.*'

Isaac Gervais is loved, even adored by his family. But anything created with one hand alone can't help but to come out clumsy or a little awkward: with his mind put before his soul, he will come across

74

as too pragmatic and coarse actually to *like*. True, he has worked hard for what he has and is prepared to fight to protect and maintain it. *'He, like us, has had to leave the kitchen in order to do so and feels he must posture and appear tough or "cool" in the face of a tougher world.'*

Coarse, he pushes away from him what he does not desire, and grabs at whatever he does. Hawking, belching, farting and spitting; I have seen him push his plate of food away from him when he wants no more. You look down at the table, to see that he does. *'I would suspect that in the unlikely case that he found himself over the River in a Roman Catholic district around Pope Street, he would throw his rubbish on the ground. Why not? – the mind might ask. Suspicious, even when he pees he guards his "Willie" from others by holding it down under a cupped hand. If you smile at him, he will stare at you while he thinks, and then decide whether or not it would be wise, or even useful, to smile back.'*

His own rough beginnings make him cautious as to where he bestows his charity. Of course, this practical intelligence includes knowing what will make him money: he is a keen businessman. You can see from his portrait that he is most comfortable when he keeps his hand in his pocket near to his hard-earned coins and IOUs. He touches that pocket when he needs to be assured, when he is troubled, and until a stranger in his presence is identified. *'Far too practical to like.'*

Old Isaac and his Mrs see themselves as too lifted by their faith to remove their clothes before partaking in sex; for it might get out of hand as things do in a farmyard. If they do, a great deal of effort will go into the art of folding their clothes – first. They have only one son.

I complain about the way in which Old Isaac brings up his only son – nothing between father and son except homage to, of course, the father. *'Do as you are told!' 'Go to the corner!'* and *'What did your father tell you?'* Now and then Christian Rebecca Philpot fills up the gap between: *'Now put it away before it is dark or someone might fall. Remember how frightened you were when you fell? Imagine how deeply it might hurt the feelings of someone old or the frail?'*

If Nature is the enemy waiting in the wings to snatch back all that Man has won from her, then only the forbearance, strategy and strength – so characteristic of the male of the species – can keep her at bay. And in the extreme assault, for instance, when men leave their assigned terrain to go out on to the sea or join a regiment to go abroad to fight, a woman's presence is considered inappropriate, and even unlucky. This is a man's world and we stand here in a man's house – 'kept by the woman'. Among Isaac's possessions is a wife, the mother of his son. She is ringed to prove this union and he can provide documents to say so, if required.

Clink, *clank.* Just as Isaac has his house, so she has her corner. As women she and the other female members of the household sit on one side of the table for their meals, and then afterwards make up their own circle in the corner by the window, where they busy themselves with sewing and lighter chores. In winter she is allowed to remain in the room to make better use of the heat. In summer she and the other women *withdraw* once the meal is completed, and make sure that the softer things are then removed so that the room's all-male atmosphere can be restored and intelligent discussion once again be resumed.

The Mrs's place, she knows, is more practically with Rebecca, the children and the other female servants. Even in chapel, the women, children and servants sit together upstairs in the gallery while the men join together as one mighty force below.

'Just look at her', I say, leading your eye to her portrait in the opposite – much smaller – alcove. *'Pleased with this portrait, her husband*

did not commission beauty. This is the face of a woman accurately recorded, whose organised, serious approach is sure to please God – as it will future generations of their descendants.'

I explain: *'It is her Protestantism that instils the room with a distinctive character – much more than any trace of her own femininity is allowed to do. Nature is kept safely at bay; no flowers, no curtains and no frills; no shadows either – nor stained glass; no deceptive smells – and in fact even the smell of boiled food here will be aired away as soon as we leave.'* Clink-clank, too much or too little. It is easy to think of the colourful Cavalier culture while forgetting the other unglamorous-on-purpose side of that same extreme: Puritan *simplicity*, with its tough and unnatural stand against dirt, sex and immorality, its war against Nature and lower forms of human behaviour.

To her, cleanliness is revealed in light and dirt hides in dark corners: it has a smell. Like most northern Protestants she leans –

after white – towards terrestrial colours, symbolic of a down-to-earth practical approach to the world, and never to the celestial, heavenly, pastels so favoured by Mediterranean Catholics. God is with her and not in the clouds; pastels suggest looking *up* instead of *in* for answers. Heavenly hues are seen as sickly, weak and vulnerable.

*Making a real
meal of survival*

78

'*See?*' To the side and posted to the wall are written instructions for house cleaning and chores – including the length of time required for dust to settle between operations. Candle ends, a penny for a servant's wage, tiny piles of tealeaves – all no doubt weighed, numbered and counted. A pie and not a joint of meat, ten apples in

the still life, two per day (for the master), until Friday next. Pewter instead of silver, delft pottery instead of finer porcelain – all this is meant to impress us with the virtue of her practical and thrifty nature. Any style or art knows to keep its head down here. Anything made too pretty by ornamentation is stored away in cabinets or displayed high up on shelves. For this reason, like other women of her age, she tends to hang pictures too high on their walls. Mrs Gervais claims that she would ideally paint every wall white, which in her case I suspect is only an excuse; using colour requires a sophistication that she apparently does not possess. White for light – and she has been presented with a kind of brass chandelier that is stripped of its former Old Faith religious embellishment. Its function is strictly *to give much light*. Her Protestantism is based on 'the word' and is conducted 'by the book', while the Old Faith is lurking in the shadows waiting to get caught. I have heard her refer to the pre-Reformation as the 'Dark Ages'.

The food she serves is kept characteristically plain. Anything kissed with a little fancy she refers to as 'confection'. She places the spoon and fork needed for the consumption of 'afters' not with the other utensils on either side of the plate, but at the top, where they are out of the way of the serious business of sustenance.

Looking around the room we can conclude that to her 'art' is God's world accurately recorded. An ancestor of photo-realism and not of impressionism. Portraits of the Gervais family and the Protestant kings they imported from Hanover, plus one still life, are all there are. *Accuracy* is her truth and her gold, and the *still life* is a predominantly Protestant art form – where the energy once dedicated to religious subjects was channelled into recording God's world as it really is. This is the joy of seventeenth-century Dutch genre painting, and what we see on the table and on the sideboards

is to Isaac what the Thanksgiving Feast is to Americans: bounty and grace. It is displayed first and then given thanks for before it is eaten. The fruit bowl displayed *at the centre* of a round table can sometimes represent to a Protestant what an altar does to a Roman Catholic, *at one end of a rectangle*.

CHAPTER SEVEN

THE ONLY WAY IS UP

A beaten-up old chamber-stick containing a lighted candle sits on the third tread of the stairs – as if an invitation. Now we hear the footsteps of a small child scuffing away somewhere above. You watch me turn and walk back to pull the door shut. *'There'* I say, to put you more at ease. Closed is the late baroque; over is our adolescence. ¶ Too much? Clink-clank – one side *OR* the other; this could drive us mad – just as it drove them to war. Instead of win *OR* lose, there must be something at the centre, something to bond, something between. In pursuit of the contentment we have lost, an instinct will have us do with our minds what we do physically if someone threatens to throw a punch: duck under or rise above. Surely we cannot duck by returning to the kitchen; for our current thinking would only contaminate so peaceful a place. We will *rise above*; like Jack and the Beanstalk, we must climb away.

In the time of this house, other Londoners of a like mind did so too. If we stand in a typical London street of terraced houses built in either the eighteenth or early nineteenth centuries, we can look up to see that the *first floor* appears to take prominence. The windows there are higher and more gracefully proportioned, sometimes even opening out on to a balcony. Indoors too, the finest, lightest and most sumptuously proportioned rooms are normally found on this higher and cleaner level: one nearer to the sun.

It was the mid-eighteenth century when the term *first floor* came into being. It is in fact the second floor; but *first* – in this case – is like the American use of the term *First Family*; the most important floor amongst many. Its technical name is *piano nobile*, or the noble floor, and it was developed by Andrea Palladio to lift grand Venetians above the damp of the Lagoon. A platform above the world, where the most civilised members of society live and entertain, while life's mundane but essential ugliness carries on below. It is the distinguishing feature of the London town house, dividing the 'smart' Georgians from the not so smart ones, who remained below to keep only a *front room*.

The accent created by the *piano nobile* makes the exterior of a row of London town houses both pleasing and elegant to the eye. The windows play with your eye, just as the *entasis* in the design of a classical column does. The ground floor is normally either stuccoed or painted white to represent the base of a column, with its windows conforming to what is approximately your own human scale. They then become larger by roughly one quarter on the first floor before

84

graduating up further to become smaller again. The whole effect comes at you – strengthens – and then goes off again with the first floor projected like a belly. It makes the house appear higher and sturdier than it actually is, and at the same time more elegant. Again, just as the same trick does for a classical column.

The staircase which awaits us is of the 'dog-leg' variety, and from where we stand we can look up to see the squared-up bend which gives it that name. The walls that encase it were once 'grained' to resemble the oak stairs in grander seventeenth-century houses, but have since gone black with generations of linseed oil and age. This must have been a part of the same baroque scheme of pretensions which included the vulgar ceiling and a floor painted with red and black lozenge shapes to resemble more expensive stone or marble. The floor is executed in perspective to make the hall appear longer than it actually is – thus drawing a visitor in. *'How the baroques loved the theatre of deception,'* I say.

Two more things before we climb. There is a type of baroque painting known as a 'vanity piece', in which a mirror is represented by a soap bubble destined either to pop or evaporate. Thus the poor creature before it, whose foolish shortsightedness allows them to establish their happiness on self-mesmerism, is doomed to long-term despair. Earlier on, when your eyes were dashing around the hall trying to identify things, you will have discovered that there is no mirror here – so near to the door – in the one place where it might be expected. No, you must not catch sight of your own reflection: not yet. For if you do, neither you nor our story can develop.

The other thing is, of course, its opposite. There is etched into a wall that haunting Radiant Eye at the top of the pyramid which backs the American one-dollar bill. It is the eye of God and the pyramid is constructed in a desert of despair from the Stones of Knowledge as a direction of escape. The idea is that if we build away from the ground we can attain a higher view of the whole picture. This is the ideal of Man's rising above his own low brutality, where the name of the game is to win OR lose, and where even if a ball is kicked at you you are made to feel that you must kick it back. Up high, for the sake of harmony and for regaining the Paradise we lost, there is hope; a reason for turning the other cheek.

So . . . UP!

So, *up* we go – '*God is (UP), Heaven is (UP), We go (UP) to Court – (UP) to London and (UP) to town. (UP) to government and (UP) to our administrators. (UP) to university – if not "sent down". Women "dress (UP)" and wear their hair "up" – to go UP; they can feel UP in a pair of high-heeled shoes. A soft-boiled egg's Up in an eggcup; a good wine – not from a tumbler – but a glass raised UP on to a stem. Up – from the smoke of the City go the merchants to the hills around London: to Blackheath, Highbury, Highgate and Hampstead. And UP the river go the Royal Court to cleaner water and fresher air; from Greenwich, to Westminster, Kensington, Richmond, Hampton Court – and then right on up to the windy shore at Windsor. Up, (UP, UP)!'* – and on to the first Landing. And do consider the word 'landing'. Wow! . . . what a sensation!

The Piano Nobile

The light which has drawn us here is that of a crystal chandelier. Ablaze overhead it reveals rich red paint and two carved door cases embellished with ivory-painted over-doors. Dotted across their top ledges are blue and white garniture in delftware and Chinese porcelain. Above that is a chalk-white rococo ceiling featuring flying putti, which – though it may be rich – is much finer than the vulgar confection downstairs. Towering upon a table as a centrepiece is a 'Queensware' – or creamware – epergne, which rises up in tiers like a wedding cake, with each tier decked with sweetmeats, some of which swing in delicate little pottery baskets suspended from all five arms. The expensive smell of marzipan and the pretty chime of a clock fill the air, as the noble face of the new Mrs Jervis's grandfather, in a full-bottomed wig, peers down at us from a portrait. (Note too – they have changed the spelling of their name from Gervais to Jervis to make it smarter and more British.) Again a painted floor, this one decorated with a compass, lies under our feet. Yes, with what we've come from still so fresh in our minds – what a sensation.

Nervous of Heights?

To see the important collections housed within the world's greatest museums and galleries, we are often made to climb a mass of stone steps – as if symbolic of the fact that they are protected and preserved from the brutality of the real world below. Getting 'real' – as they say, any such delicacy as surrounds us here would never survive one night down in the street any more than a real work of art would survive without being stolen, vandalised or sold. Those things that stand out from Nature are picked on and destroyed – like the brightly coloured canary set loose into the wild. Nature is low; art and sophistication shelter the high. The word sophistication means just that: unnatural, perverted away from the natural state. It is the way a cockney sees London's Knightsbridge. *'How magnificent!'* – Visitors often gasp at what greets them here. What would happen? – I see them think – what if it were *they* who accidentally caught hold of that epergne and sent it crashing – sweetmeats and all – down the stairs? Imagine the noise, the mess . . . the *embarrassment*!

Your fear of embarrassment is purposely engineered by this higher, grander setting, for it is essential to our journey's refinement. You see, it is to avoid embarrassment that, like tightrope walkers, we must develop our natural ability for balance. We must *manner* our thinking and behaviour, by either *widening* or *narrowing* what we already are. If at this new height we do not, then we will fall down.

Looking about us, I say, *'Never was there a Time when Man prided himself on being so* unnatural . . . *Look, everything around us up here is a perversion away from what is real into what is really a safe distance – ritual level – representation.'* Pointing up to the 'rococo' ceiling. A style created by the eighteenth century to redesign Nature for itself, turning away from the formal unyielding plan, based so solidly on human physical symmetry, to a stylized version created in its opposite: a-symmetry. *'The porcelain, too, is still only the tarted-up delft pottery we saw downstairs, but covered with a thick white glaze – like make-up – and then painted with blue decoration in order to appear like the higher-grade finer Chinese version.'* And as for the glass crystal chandelier: the very symbol of *un*naturalness to us today? Is not the first thing we do with a crystal to hold it up to the light? The result is a collection of stones suspended around a light source. We circle and gawk, like . . . two moths.

Quite frankly all this *unnaturalness* is a relief, and is already at work

in providing the safe and confident setting we need as the haven for refinement. *Up here* is a kind of artificial wonderland, with no fear of brutality, no one trying to sell us anything or 'come on' to us, away from kicking balls, the 'bully', and with no one to laugh.

But the first floor is a minefield laid with little reminders of your clumsy, clodhopping origins. Things are purposely placed a little too precariously to one side so that you may brush up against them if you try to sweep past too gloriously. Seashells are placed beneath carpets to make an uncomfortable crunching sound should you begin to strut, and a door without a latch awaits your bid to appear cool by leaning up against it. As an artist my canvas is your imagination, and left on your own – unimpressed and fearless of social embarrassment – would you ever play along with me tonight?

High Minded

The idea of lifting one's self *above* the real world is a noble and urban aspiration, not a bourgeois one. The latter tend to sprawl horizontally in their quest for comfort and convenience, as they do across the beach, across their lounge suites and sofas. The sideways withdrawal from urban brutality gave birth to our suburbs. In old Amsterdam town houses the burghers (natives of a flat terrain) began by withdrawing *back* from the canals to their beautiful room, or 'mooie kamer', which was positioned up a few steps (sometimes called an 'op kamer', or 'up room'). And until the elevator was invented to make the penthouse possible, the Americans too – with so much space available – simply ran away from their cities and up to new houses built in the 'heights' or on 'nob hill'. Even in America's European-styled East Coast town houses the best rooms were seldom lifted, but merely raised above the street enough to allow passing citizens a glimpse of the householders' finest ceilings, over-doors, and chimneypieces.

However, in the ancient walled-in cities of orthodox Europe, the nobility, needing to be close to the Court and safely locked up at night within the city walls, stayed put, and lifted themselves above the darkness and stench by developing the 'upstairs–downstairs' town house.

So – the *piano nobile* is to be responsible for our own nobler intelligence. Up here we can safely remove our armour and allow a sense of gentleness and self-discipline to emerge and advise us how best to adjust to what is conducive to society as a whole. The volume, pitch and tone of our voices, our accents and postures, the way we wish to dress, smell and appear to others, will all soon change. I soften my voice to add, *'And, if I might suggest that . . . your expression:*

the one that some would refer to as "attitude" – and which you still wear from downstairs: it is too defensive . . . suggests a restricted view. Up here – it's altitude, not attitude.'

Standing to Reason

'*Listen!*' I say, turning to face the door on our right. Beyond it we hear a young male voice raised in conversation – still only of men, but one that for some reason we prefer the tone of. It sounds *reasonable*, with no one single voice making us either cringe, shrug or rise to take a side. A conversation rich with fellowship, which it would be agreeable, even fun, to join. Either our imaginations, or Time itself, have finally started to grow up.

'*Listen!*' I say, turning to face the door on our right. Beyond we hear a young male voice speaking clearly amid much rowdiness. '*Isaac's son, Edward Jervis,*' I whisper. '*Listen!*' We look at each other before bending our heads closer.

'*. . . Old Faith or New? Can it matter? For surely both must exist! It is geography, gentlemen, and not religion. Look at what we drink . . .*' – we hear him say to a few hecklers. '*From the south of Europe up to the north, just think how it changes: red wine; then up to beer and ale; then on up further and it's whisky, vodka and schnapps. Portuguese wine has to be fortified with spirit to make it into the "port" that suits our palate here in England. Is it not true of religion, too?*'

If we relax in the north, we may not survive! Geography – Men! . . . Reason! – not just Old Faith or New. Think high!

'*And – in philosophy . . .*' and the other men begin to hurl *woooos* at the wise old man of twenty years of age. '*Was it not old Lord Bolingbroke's theory that maintained in his* Idea of a Patriot King *that it is a duty of a monarch to be strong – at the centre – in order to hold together two naturally opposing, and potentially warring sides? And have you noticed – in politics – how both Whig and Tory have stopped waging open war on each other and established themselves as "parties" – each with their own version of the common public good as their billing? One day, it will be on its merit – and not just bribes – that each party will win its return to power.'*

'And, was it not Edward Jervis who married an Anglican and Tory in order to rule Spitalfields?' – we hear someone add.

With the fire popping and crackling, glasses clinking and the uncorking of even more bottles, we find ourselves having to bend closer together in order to hear more clearly through the door.

'In music . . .', and Edward sings the word in a shaky E-flat in an attempt to cover over the last impertinent observation, *'in music we make it seem that the melody itself is becoming more and more important: more important, it might sometimes seem, than the mathematical rules of counterpoint harmony which we were taught so diligently. Is it not like that electricity machine we walked over to see at Reverend Wesley's? Where the two destructive forces of lightning are moderated to become "electricity" – with some useful effects. In our time, gentlemen, have we not witnessed the effects in medicine of treating "like with like". In particular the case which has amazed us all with regard to smallpox – where by putting a small quantity of the evil stuff into our blood, our body prepares its own defence.'*

I begin, *'Visitor, if I recall correctly from my own adolescence . . .'* But there I halt to rephrase. *'If I recall correctly from school, in the Age of Enlightenment, Reason emerged, to find a time. From the sound of it, something of the Age of Reason might still exist,'* I return my eyes to the door. I nod forward, *'. . . in there.'*

CHAPTER EIGHT

COMING OF AGE

A sharp thud startles us as something on the other side of the door crashes to the floor. Now a loud yawn, a shout, and someone attempts a song which ends abruptly. Silence. ¶ *'Visitor, quickly! Open the door – catch it before it fades!'* ¶ In the same instant we reach for the handle and hurriedly throw open the door. We gaze into a haze; at the place where it happened; where Reason took hold. ¶ It is another painting: its sitters so much closer than those downstairs, with one still lingering about. *'Shoo!'* – I clap my hands. *'There! Gone; now, go on in.'* – I whisper with a nudge, *'Enter the morning after, 1761.'* ¶ As we step forward, your eyes lift immediately to the painting done a quarter of a century before, that hangs above the mantelpiece. Bored to death with compound intelligence, I do not wish to hear a name so I say it for you: *'William Hogarth.'* You must blur your eyes, for the tobacco smoke hanging in the air is making everything a little too difficult to see. By design? Having a name and date to work with I see the first suggestion of a smile come to your face; you are no longer lost in time. With the painting as a point of mutual interest, I comment on how interesting it is that a frame does not separate it from us.

'The scene is held up there by a simple wooden moulding . . . almost as if on hearing our approach the whole party retreated to the wall and froze there in an attempt to hide . . . as if to tease us into making us imagine it.'

The painting shows us the scene we have just heard. It is four a.m., the closing minutes of an eighteenth-century bachelor assembly. Though you peer about you, you do not see what you are supposed to see, not yet. For, hidden before you in this room is something that makes higher things *high*, and by the lack of it, keeps lower things *low*.

True enough, it would appear that the painting is only held in place by surface tension; at any moment it might break, go liquid and pour down around us to consume us in its own smoky reality. *'Look! . . .'* – I point to the chair we heard fall, the man we heard yawn and to the one we heard begin a song. *'It could be the very scene.'*

The sensation is often described as spellbinding. The atmosphere seems to force your attention from commodities and into a state between. There is something more here, something too familiar, too poignant and *all too relative* to ignore. What is it?

'Quickly . . . before it fades!'

Getting the Picture?

How it happens will happen differently to different people. But it usually begins with you noticing pieces of broken clay pipe lying on the floor beneath your feet which you fear you might harm. When you reach forward you discover that they are not lying on the floor at all, but are in fact *sunken into the floor*. Everything else is rational; this is not. The way the light is positioned draws you back to the Hogarth painting for help, to find that there are three pipes in the painting, too. The same shape and size, the same position within the room.

Then, to the rhythm of the clock, it all begins to fall into place: tick-tock – and you begin to reverse out of the painting and into the room. At the same time, you also begin to advance from the room up and into the painting. Back and forth, tick and tock, the picture and the room in which you sit are one. The men are gone, but you have taken their place and are sitting amongst what they left behind.

It takes some minutes to comprehend the extent and strength of this new reality. But there it all is. The punchbowl with the same curly piece of lemon peel hanging over its lip. The same overturned candlestick with a puddle of wax spilled over the tablecloth; the reflection from the candle on the side of that very bottle; even the way the firelight dusts across the folds in the linen cloth: all the same. There it all is; and I know I can trust your late twentieth-century trained-to-be-critical eye to notice that the jacket of the gentleman who previously sat on the left of the canvas is still hanging directly before you over the back of the same chair; that his newspaper – with the same date – still projects from its pockets. If you still have it in you to be critical, now is your last chance. find *that*

wig, find *that* jacket and each of *those* tricorne hats; exhaust it – *all*: use it *all* up. 'My *God!*' – I hear you say from the other side of the door – '*Yes!* . . . *only the console table is missing.*'

However, more important – but still unspotted – is what we have risen up to find: the precious substance that floats in the air between your eye and each object. Just as the varnish helps to bond together the components in a painting to make them come together as a whole, so too does the atmosphere in the air of this room. It has its own colour and is one of my own recipes. The Dutch call it 'gezelligheid': a kind of smoky, cinnamon brown haze which harbours warmth, cosiness and life, and is a characteristic of the interior scenes they once had a genius for painting. Here, still rich with the waves of heat and draught, with the smell of tobacco, tallow smoke, wood ash and punch; the *air* is still rich with life. In fact, is it – the *space between* things – not as strong as, if not stronger, than anything else? So, by design, it is.

The Space Between is the invisible, shared third element that lies between any two sides. It contains all we have in common with anyone else. Good or bad, it is the place where sharing *being alive* happens. Without its recognition, there can only be single-sidedness, selfish ignorance and war. Like the varnish over the painting, a healthy space between brings together, bonds and then protects the whole picture.

Around you sounds begin to paint a picture in a circle, making you its centre. A barking dog takes your ear outside, where a new dawn is being announced by a chorus of birds. Inside, behind you, a caged canary begins to compete, while servants are heard starting their work: glasses are collected and washed, and somewhere a floor is being swept. All of this has woken one of the Jervis children, whom you can hear fussing about on the landing. The new Mrs Jervis, with a voice as balanced and pleasing as her husband's, has just been heard for the first time. Round and round: surface tension dissolves and it's all around you.

You see? What you may have heard happens in this house, has happened to you. It is all quite scientific – all about *three*. 1 you; 2 a room; and 3 a space between. And when you say '*My God!*' you have to draw it into your lungs, so – whether you see or you don't – believe me, you are *there*. From the inside out, the Age of Reason is now.

A bell is tolling to say that someone in the parish has died in the night. Horses and other traffic are beginning to cart their loads over the stone streets out front, while at the back a carpet is being beaten and a voice announces that the weather is beginning to change. The whole picture is beginning to balance in the round.

THE SPACE BETWEEN

You sit gazing into the space between. Think what a difference it would make to the world if our young were taught to see any subject in three parts, with the wellbeing of all at the centre. Someone once described music as the space between notes. Astronomers often see the universe in the pull of *total control* on the one side and *total chaos* on the other; economists look to the space between *supply* and *demand* to determine value and price. Should we not do the same? What good is a clock if the tick and the tock cannot come together to tell the time? ¶ I lift one of the long clay pipes before us on the table and use it to point to the place of our mutual embarkation; from

where we are about to travel into our newly discovered territory. We are about to set off on what was known in the eighteenth century as a 'discourse', a time to 'philosophise'.

'Look, . . . see the smouldering wick?' I point to the brass candlestick on the table and to its tiny socket, in which there burns a flickering pool of wax. You look; we look; and then we both sneak a glimpse of the Hogarth painting to check that there is a parallel. Sure enough, the same candlestick; not actually flickering, but with a smoke stream rising out of its socket instead.

Suddenly the flame heaves up its last flicker and then goes out. And yes, a smoke stream is sent trailing into the air. *'See? Watch it glide up – not down – but up, into the air.'* I ask you to close your eyes.

'For some God-given reason – the smoke stream is beginning to perform for us. Do not open your eyes,' I insist, *'but take it from me, that it has begun to dance, twist, pirouette and tie itself into a bow – and even mock itself – like a genie from a bottle!'* I go silent so that you may watch. I see you smile.

'All this is so exceptional, so unnatural, that it manages to take us away from ourselves and out to it – instead! There, before us, is something above what is natural: a form of "sophistication".'

I allow you time to think: theatre, opera, ballet and rock concerts; nightclubs, sports or religious services – the most sophisticated of which draw you right out of yourself. Things that take you – *up,* but not down.

I lead you higher. *'The smoke stream is now becoming so sophisticated and balanced that others join with others to give it their attention. A desire is developing to make it more widely shared: to draw it – take photographs – to somehow record and preserve it for the future. People are willing to pay to see it: there is a value and it even has its own market. This is* "art".'

A pedestal, a column and a capital, and higher we go.

'Impressed, others join with others to lean and develop in the direction cast by its example. It stands on its own, and a "culture" *is born.'*

Starting from Here

An old story. A man was once asked, *'Which is the way to Dublin?'* To which, after thinking for several seconds and looking around him to scratch one ear, he replied, *'Well, if I were you, I wouldn't start from here.'*

Starting from here is one of my specialities, and if a student of time asked me: *'Which is the way to the Age of Reason?'* – I would tell them without any hesitation at all to start from here.

Few visitors can actually explain what has happened to them during their visit to the house simply because what happens for some does not, will not and cannot happen for others. Two things are happening at the same time: one is a *tour* of an old house to inform you about what you see and identify; the other is an adventure of the imagination. If at the end of the evening, a visitor says to me, *'Very interesting,'* or *'Absolutely fascinating,'* or *'What was that colour in the dressing room?'* – then fine, I know that they listened, looked and were probably well entertained, but no more. If – on the other hand – a departing visitor is unable to speak and touches my arm to slip away, then I know that something more complex has occurred. That, somewhere during the evening, they have left the others behind to turn a corner and find the house's pair of heroes, Edward and Elizabeth Jervis.

The Plot

This is a room conducive to Reason: there are no 'sides' waiting to jump out at you and take you off-centre: the central space is too strong.

This house does not believe that compound intelligence is the natural state of Man's thinking, but that it is only a short-cut compromise for the sake of mass education and for the passing of examinations in order to get jobs. It is what I – if only a crackpot artist – am up against with so many of my visitors. On the occasions when I have entertained in this room privately, I have often been shocked to see those who are known as 'shapers' – politicians and 'thinkers' – suddenly become like retarded children as they fail to name and number things which are unfamiliar to them. Sometimes when they fail they will actually seize up or become almost belligerent. One art critic, apparently numb to any beauty outside a frame, tidied the contents of this table into neat little piles for washing up. A famous sculptor and Royal Academian ate my still lives whenever I left the room. One of the great minds of our day smoked a clay pipe only to sit staring into the fire to make the same contribution to every subject. *'I don't know, but I have a book at home that would tell me.'* These are all the cool people to whom fashion tells us to trust our destinies.

In a rounder spirit of balance I should add that this same room brings out the very best in 'problem' students – those who I suspect are petty East End criminals and even drug dealers. Jack-the-lads-right-on-top use all that they have to work it all out almost as quickly as they enter, with energy and imagination to spare. So much so that some can even work out why it is unwise and unethical to tilt the balance by stealing from it. Surely the world must be wasting its resources if these people are locked up while the minds of our blinkered leaders, constipated by education, are the ones I've seen walk into lampposts?

So the house has a mission, and it believes that the natural state of human intelligence is not – like a painting – *flat* or *square*, but like this room it extends out and all around us. The house plots to work its magic to ensure that each visitor goes away with that perception. It may have already begun to happen to you.

A Mess: in the Best of Taste

The difference between rubbish and the bricks, stone, concrete and metal that make up our streets is that the latter are structured to balance from a spine, and will therefore hold together, whereas the former is wild. But if you do what you were warned not to do and examine in detail the mess around you here, you will find that it is not rubbish at all, but that each item is crafted to appear 'tasteful'. The words *Georgian* and *taste* are almost synonymous.

Just what was the eighteenth century's secret for pleasing the eye? Surely it was, like the views we overheard of Edward Jervis's company, a developed sense of moderation for the sake of a whole: a balance that pleases Mankind by striking a chord with his own form, weight and construction. It was almost as if the Georgians brought things together and then bonded them by employing the golden rule, '*Do unto others as you would have them do unto you.*'

A state of regulated harmony is now their quest – a state called 'Just Right'.

A New Perspective

I begin to show you the room – but this time from the inner space outwards. Encasing you here are walls constructed of wood panelling with *sunken* fields: that is, the fields of the panels are set inward – or away from you – whereas those of the seventeenth century were *raised* to be *bolection* (meaning bold), with the inner panel curved out higher than the frame. The room's contours curve back too and, whereas the paint downstairs contained linseed oil to protect it and give it a gloss, here it is flattened to become 'dead', so that your eye reaches out to a hue instead of having to deal with a scatter of glossy reflections. Chairs here are no longer so tall that they fall back, but are pruned of the ornament or pretensions which separate them from those they seat. These newer chairs do not deceive our eye by covering over their inferior beechwood origins with thick black 'Japanning' to resemble exotic and expensive ebony, but are made of honest imported mahogany. A wood so tightly grained that it will not disintegrate, but will hold together actually to improve with age. Nothing too bold is waiting to jump out and rob our attention. Hence our new behaviour to one another and the reasonable conversation. And hear? The clock does not limp – *clink OR clank*, but *ticks and tocks* . . . just right.

Looking over at the window, I say, *'Reason is indeed taking control. Heat and smoke rise – and draughts and Nature lurk low to the ground. Can children – still crawling so low to the ground – not fall out of the windows? See? – No more: instead of windows that open out from the centre – as did old casements in the seventeenth century, to get caught by wind or by fire – Reason has asked us to invent the "sash" window instead. It moves up and down so that the top or bottom half can be either lifted or lowered to whatever is reasonable. And if floors are often so crooked that they make four table legs wobble, then surely three legs – or "tripod" – will straddle. So the reasonable Georgians developed, built and bought their tripod tables.'* Seeing you caught by the spirit of Reason, I continue, *'And as for pissing: outside – no longer the medieval open central gutter to which those on both sides of a lane pushed their refuse and sewerage. Now . . . streets with a pavement on either side for pedestrians – each with its own gutter for drainage (soon to have drains) and with a common space between: the roadway itself! So civilised! . . . no more is it, "I win so YOU lose", but now we ALL win.'* A fresh look around the room, and yes, things are certainly more intelligent. Reason is indeed in charge.

Tick AND Tock

If the Shakespearean actor obeys the verse, he will never have to plan where to breathe when he delivers his lines. Shakespeare was a good poet, not a bad one: *'To be?* (breathe in) *Or not to be?* (breathe out) – *That is the question'* (new breath). It fits. Similarly it was the 'just right' target in Georgian cabinet-making that made their furniture co-ordinate so neatly with the dimensions of their rooms and houses. Any fine piece of 'occasional' furniture was normally of just the right dimensions to be transported through doors, up and down stairs, or conveniently stored inside cupboards. Hence the need for all those footmen and servants.

Under this room's spell your mind might suddenly feel the urge to join with the mid-Georgians to tidy things up: both inside your head and out. To slam on the brakes and cringe at the sight of things that are 'vulgar'. Would we not now wish to turn a heavy and clumsy old baroque eyesore of a house into a lighter and more refined piece of architecture on lines of the aforementioned Palladio – thus making it *Palladian*? Might we not employ Lancelot 'Capability' Brown to sweep away and replace all those old formal gardens with newly created 'natural landscapes'? If left to us, would we not bend the Long Water in Kensington Gardens and Hyde Park – once straightened to be formal – back again into a *Serpentine*? We could ask that artist of yours, the one whose name you know by heart – Mr Hogarth – if he might pause from engraving his satirical pictures on the theme of *too much, too little – too late*, to do something more interesting and stylish with the straight line? Have him bend it in just such a way that the human eye perceives its elegance; into his famous *Line of Beauty*.

The aim is to become balanced, to become timeless – or *classical*.

And so to the perfect tick AND tock. I see your gaze go out, not only to a chair, but to a piece of silver, a china dish, a piece of silk woven by Edward Jervis here in Spitalfields. We are in the mood of thought, and taste, that some recognise as *understatement*. That is, '*I could do . . . but my finer self somehow tells me not to.*'

Into the space between we go to find – him. I lift the same clay pipe from the table to begin conducting and orchestrating the sophistication of the unseen. I point first to the barber's basin and pole, to make it into *Edward Jervis's* barber's basin and pole. The red stripes on a barber's pole, I explain, represent blood – and the service of *bleeding* performed by the barber for the sake of *his* better health (new blood, new life), while the white advertises clean bandages; the stick itself is gripped by the person being bled. Hair is for protection: it is low, so what remains of Edward's hair must be neatly cut, removed or groomed. His head is then covered with a wig, not for the sake of vanity, but for the sake of the company he shares with those in this higher circle who wear the same. The little bundle of parsley is to clean his breath. '*You see*', I say to your imagination, while knowing too well that while some part of your mind is still concerned with identifying 'things', another part is busy creating Edward Jervis, '*the Space Between is more important to him than anyone or anything on either side.*'

And now to his punch bowl and its five ingredients: water, spirit, spice, lemon and sugar. Punch is a Hindustani word for five, and the little glass sugar crushers before you are there so that each of young Edward's guests might sweeten to taste, as we do our own cup of tea today. His reason is – again – the Space Between; for if the concoction is too sweet, then not all of his company will drink together, and so the meeting will be left divided. I add, '*If Reason fails, we can at least imagine Edward Jervis "punched" – with five fingers – in the jaw.*'

Punch means *five:* there are always five ingredients . . .

Living with Taste

I say, *'Man's finest discipline: Reason. Unlike Old Isaac's front parlour, which lobbied only one side of our intelligence to paint his image, this room persuaded us to imagine his son Edward with our natural gift for moderation. He will be gentler: Edward Jervis is to be a "gentleman", even appear physically finer than his father,'* – I narrow my eyes in order to look back and see more clearly – *'a man whose posture and expression were moulded by the extreme stand he took against the world. There . . . see?'* I smile with satisfaction. *'Nothing too big; nothing too small; no pigeon toes, no "push and pull" – no "attitude"; still Protestant – but with no "piles".'*

Such are his beginnings, and Edward will slip out into his time not to stand out, but, like others of his generation, to dress and behave in such a way that blends in harmony with his age. His clothing will be less flamboyant in cut, colour and pattern than previously, and will aim more to the centre than to the extreme. He will no longer wish to steal the show from the fairer sex, but will delight in seeing women emerge, for the first time, as the more beautifully dressed.

Looking over at a very sleek wine bottle; more elegant and less defensive than the onion-shaped affairs in our adolescent baroque, I say, 'Maybe it is only by coincidence . . . but somehow – from here, whatever I recall from the mid-eighteenth century seems to boil down to being much finer than before; from their clothing to the simplest balustrade.'

So, will our *gentleman* spit? Can a gentleman spit? Will we hear Edward Jervis break wind? Belch? Cough or – even if he can help it – yawn, sniff or sneeze? Or are such things related to a too basic distrust of Nature, and therefore too 'low' for what we imagine? Is their expulsion not often part of the same attention-seeking that was so much a part of the 'show off' individuality of our own youth? To see him spit or fart might make us cringe. Thank goodness history assured us that in the very same way that Edward Jervis is an improvement, so his own society also approved.

I point out that new buildings are being constructed of yellow London stock brick to resemble stone, rather than the eye-catching, light-tinting, flashy red brick with white paint of the old houses of Restoration London, this one included. As you look over at Edward's new toned-down London-yellow jacket, I can see you compare it with his father's bright old woollen red one. You are seeing the London you know, but from a different perspective.

I say – to myself, '*Now, what to call this culture of people whose lives are led by a talent for Reason? Who are governed by careful moderation and the necessary thrift it takes to balance and ensure their safe prosperity? A class above, below and between: I know . . . a "Middle Class".*'

Our man's tastes will regulate him away from extremes and in the direction of easing the world towards a better balance. He will believe in Catholic emancipation and the new societies for the promotion of the arts and sciences; he will give handsomely to the Foundling Hospital and promote Sunday Schools for the children of the poor. His fear of extremes will make him listen to his instincts to ease the injustices and poverty that might suddenly turn to readjust themselves, thus destroying all – with revolution – in their wake. All this is considered – as a geologist might worry about the growing weight of the polar ice caps. Governed by Reason, our man joined in with a 'history' that did the same.

Hearing footsteps descending the stairs, I reach forward and gently open the door. We peer out on to the landing – to where the chandelier has been snuffed. Yet in that semi-darkness how imposing the door to the Withdrawing Room appears, its ivory paint glowing in a more subtle light – almost like the softest gold. We look at each other: are we ready? Somehow I think we are.

CHAPTER TEN

IN CELEBRATION OF HARMONY, A WITHDRAWING ROOM

We enter a large rectangular room to receive a wonderful sensation: one of peace, order and harmony. The draught created by opening the door has sent the lights of the twenty-four candles mounted in silver sticks and gilt brackets into a flurry of reflections and diamond-like sparkles. We are somehow drawn to the centre, where we find ourselves contained within fine proportions and a formal symmetry which make the room appear much larger and grander than it could possibly be. Walls of dark green; a

noble door case, a carved chimneypiece and its three window surrounds – each painted in ivory white and hung with red silk satin; relief ornaments and carvings coated with gold leaf; this room is almost breathtakingly rich. As one young art student recently exclaimed upon entering it, *'Holy Shit!'*

Again, we are reminded of the word taste, for we stand amidst something which our new, enlightened state has trained us to seek: nothing *too much*, nothing *too little*; this room is *just right*: it is the eighteenth-century ideal. And it is the chord struck with the symmetry, proportions and weight of our own human form that tells us so. Rich and yet uncluttered, with any ornament carefully balanced by equal amounts of plain space, so that everything has the space it needs to breathe. I ask you to join me in partially closing our eyes to see how, to any one thing on one side, there is something standing in reply on the other. If anything more should be added or subtracted, the sensation will be lost. Here is the Golden Rule in a room: with each side regulated to do unto the other what – ideally – it would wish the other side to do to it. Yes, the sensation is *Harmony*.

What we are doing in this room is what the eighteenth century called 'withdraw'. That is, to withdraw from the real world below: from the table, from business, sport and chores, and also from the private rooms upstairs in which the house's occupants sleep, cleanse and dress. With the coming of nightfall and the day's work completed, the Jervises can dress and withdraw in company to celebrate the night in this finer setting.

High

The room's semi-grandeur is intended to arouse more of the enlightening instinct that we felt when arriving upon the *piano nobile*. That is, the aspiring twitch that made us look at each other and then at ourselves to modify and refashion what we were, to become potential partners instead of remaining perennial foes. The same conditioning that would make us dress up, hold wind, switch off a mobile phone, soften a view or lower our voice – as we would in a public gallery, library or museum. Here, as in a civic or religious building, the space between comes *first*, and the room's formal dignity reminds us of this.

Architecturally, this room amounts to a miniature classical temple; and had photography been invented by the Georgians – and

this room been recorded – their first step would have been to empty the room of all its contents. Revealed then is a rectangular box with its wooden panelling arranged vertically from floor to ceiling to stand formally, like lines of *columns* mounted on *pedestals*, to form the *dado*, and then crowned at the top with *capitals*, represented by the *cornice*. The linear effect projects the same formal seriousness as pinstripes on a suit: it is as almost as if all four walls are standing to attention, like guardsmen, to salute us. Appropriately, I see that you are responding to them, or rather to the room, with a style of dignity and reverence to match.

Men and Women

Now the atmosphere in the Smoking Room next door was, despite any high talk of Reason, a lopsided affair in that it was wholly masculine, with not a single feminine touch anywhere in sight.

'Hush! Listen! . . . Out on the landing!' On the very same morning after, with her husband imagined still suffering in his bed, we hear Mrs Edward Jervis, pictured hand on hip, pausing with Rebecca at the Smoking Room door to contemplate the mess left behind by last night's revellers:

'We should be thankful for what remains in one piece,' we hear her say. *'The very idea: ten men in a single room without the company of a single woman! Too much, too little, too late – all so barbaric! And so old-fashioned!'* – Mrs Edward Jervis.

So 'old-fashioned'. Visitor, what we have just heard Mrs Jervis implying is a natural phenomenon which is now recognised by the enlightened of the eighteenth century just as it was by the ancient Greeks and Romans. That two genders must come together to create culture, just as they must do to create a child. Art, culture and civilisation are born *between*. Society is the blend of men and women, with the two genders' 'ordained roles' left downstairs below. And where more perfect than a Drawing Room to break down the partition and bring together the sexes.

If we think about it: are *extremes* of either femininity or masculinity ever the ingredients for the company we imagine in 'cultured' circles? No, not here, nor in general.

Yes, the Ancient Greeks blurred the line between masculinity and femininity – particularly in sculpture – on purpose, to harden up what was soft (woman), and soften up what was hard (men), so that they might *induce* culture. This new attitude, and the fashion for mixing the sexes, made the eighteenth century develop its taste for good and pleasing manners; something which happened for the same reasons in France one hundred years earlier.

I am watching you in relation to the room, and so far – so good. The way you sit has become more elegant, less offensively casual, and you have stopped leaning up against walls. I, too, have softened my voice and become less arrogant. (Oh – yes I have!) It is not that the room is asking us to change, but by impressing us it has won us over; we want to be a part: be at our best. The Age of Reason was refinement's time and the room is creating that spell.

Cohesion

Despite its formality, the Drawing Room is more inviting, generous and comfortable than any room so far. A good carpet under our feet, rich curtains and upholstery – this room has been softened by a woman's touch.

'Ah! There it is!' I turn excitedly and point behind us to the centre of the back wall, to the very console table missing from the scene by

Hogarth which we have only so recently walked out of. Above it, on the wall, hangs a handsome looking-glass of tortoise shell and gilt, flanked on either side by a pair of richly embossed silver wall sconces.

This very formal arrangement, a *triad of three things*, is a reminder of the days when such rooms were sad places of female exile and is descended from what was the lady of the household's dressing table. Here the women were parked with their own vanity as their amusement – while they waited for the men, who, if they could still see straight, *might* decide to arrive later. So segregated were the cultures of the two sexes that sometimes they developed in such opposite directions as to become bizarre. Ladies of the Stuart Court would often amuse themselves by sitting in circles to tell each other sentimental stories while shedding tears into little bottles so that they might compare them afterwards and see who had won at being most feminine.

However, this antiquated arrangement placed a useful seed in the male subconscious. The desired effect is like that of a football player coming out a shower after a match to find a woman sitting in a corner of the changing room sewing. No matter how much he pretends to play down her presence or turn it into a joke, the manner of his behaviour will, for sure, soon begin to soften. The arrangement announces that while the house itself may belong to the husband, and is only kept by his wife, the Drawing Room is a woman's domain. Here the shoe is on the other foot, and any visiting male will therefore have to play by her rules. *From here* the idea of a Smoking Room and all the male things associated with it, should make clearer sense.

Here, Women are the Hosts, Men their Guests.
The Effect is Gentility.

Squaring Up and Rounding Off

'You know that sketch by Leonardo de Vinci?' I ask as I rise to my feet to face you. By extending both arms and making them glide up and down like the wings of a flapping chicken, I then say: *'You see? Everything that Man builds ends up looking just like him; and in this room this is more emphasised than in most. The symmetry of your body matches the room's symmetry; its scale, volume and proportions. We fit here.*

'The same sketch draws attention to the human body in relation to taste and with it to the circle *and the* square, *which represent the extreme contours of our bodies – just as they do the rudiments of literally everything we build. Look around you,'* I say, while gesturing in a circle at literally everything here in order to illustrate my point. *'See? Just like our bodies, a manmade world is comprised of the same variations, all* between *the circle and the square.'*

Constantly amazed to find how few people have ever worked this out, I allow you time to let it soak in and see for yourself how absolutely universal it is. Then I watch you lift your hand to begin examining the rectangular segments – with the circular ends – of your fingers.

'You see, the square *(or rectangle) is symbolic of the straight way in which males – in particular – aim to organise and negotiate their world. In the case of the rectangle, there must be a hierarchy, someone at the top, to lead. Its virtue is a figure called* "Strength". *Mr Jervis is responsible for the no-nonsense, squarer features here, as men normally are in architecture and the building trade. He regards the heat source, or hearth – situated at one end of the room – as its centre.'*

And on the other hand: *'The* circle *represents our godlier ideals of fellowship and fraternity.'* Its virtue is a figure holding a wheel with a fixed hub, called *'Constancy.'* I explain how if Mr Jervis has built a box for his family's protection, his wife would be expected to create a circle of life within it, and that he sees the talents associated with

129

the circle as nesting ones. Mrs Jervis would argue that the centre of the room is not the warmth of the hearth, but in the warmth of the family or social circle which she keeps alive with herself as its hub. For this reason he would seat his special guest at the hearth, while *she* would seat hers beside her at the tea table.

I explain how the *box* is Man's first piece of furniture, used to store what more of his possessions there are than he can actually wear. Everything else in his strategy really starts from there: Mr Jervis's very first material possession was the box that he made, in which he still keeps his Bible. He would march into battle within a battalion formed into a square (making corners for protection), and though he would 'box' or wrestle in what he calls a *ring*, somewhere along the line his species tidied it up into a square. All the while his wife would sew in, and be part of, a *circle*. You will see his eye go out to the overall shape of a garment; and hers go immediately to the stitching around the outer edge; again like a hen tending to the nest. There is an old-fashioned saying that hanging pictures can ruin a marriage. Now we know why.

So in this room 'taste' is no longer a mystery, but is almost scientifically regulated. It is what is *squared up* and *rounded off* for the sake of the space between. And done so here, not just by the mind, but by a man *AND* a woman, with each other in mind.

Your eyes begin to wander. What often strikes visitors as most memorable are the swags of walnuts and beechnuts which Mrs Jervis has constructed and hung across her husband's no-nonsense post and lintel panelling. The rounding effect has, by festooning, eased its formal severity in a style reminiscent of the great decorative woodcarver, Grinling Gibbons.

In doing so, Mrs Jervis has inadvertently tapped into the origin of all architectural decoration. In ancient times women must have decorated the temples for festivals in the same way that they are traditionally responsible for the flowers in our churches today. To get their contribution right in our minds we should think of our own houses when they are first decorated for Christmas; and then the reverse sensation: the starkness when the decorations are removed. For both probably gave birth to the idea of picking up a chisel and carving decoration out of stone or wood to make what were once *real* flowers, husks, ropes, pegs, and so on permanent.

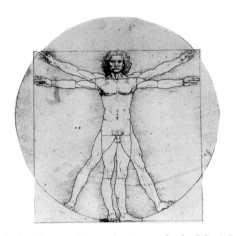

Proportions of the Human Figure by Leonardo da Vinci. The human body is the place where the synthesis of earth (square) and heaven (circle) occur. Our instinct for Divine Providence *leans toward the* circle, whereas our yearnings for Free Will lean towards practicality and the manmade square. However, the whole picture is that both man and woman – Protestant and Catholic – exist *between,* and we are blessed in hearing the circle within us sometimes ask the square, *'How can we believe in God and still go on doing such things?'* And the square ask the circle, *'What good are our prayers and high ideals when what is so clearly needed is . . . ?'* The answer is always in the bull's eye at the centre.

If we give Mr Jervis a piece of rope he will immediately begin testing it for its strength and thinking how he might use it. Mrs Jervis, in contrast, would immediately inspect it to see if it is in need of repair. If left alone with it long enough, she might even tidy it up by weaving the frayed strands at either end into something resembling a tassel.

Mrs Jervis has succeeded where her husband is doomed to fail: she gives him the softness which – as a human being – he craves. Softness is Mrs Jervis's best card: her strongest weapon and shield in dealing with her husband and the opposite sex. If he shouts, she cries, and this – you can be sure – clears the way for getting more of what she wants. If, on the other hand, as a woman, she tried to stand up to him by using a female version of his own male strength, he might simply clout her and knock her out cold.

As part of the same conspiracy we see that Mrs Jervis has gone to town in dressing the room's windows with silk arranged *in situ*, with pins. Not so much curtains but elaborate pelmets to doll up and mark the border between the wider, colder world outside, and to advertise the warmer, safely protected, cosier one she has created within. These *French* curtains conceal her father-in-law's crudely practical wooden shutters. Previously, if curtains existed at all, they were to keep back the draughts and followed the straighter, more masculine line of architecture. Their curves here have become unashamedly feminine! Again, Edward Jervis's blind eye leaves his wife triumphant; for while he refuses to admit even to seeing any such thing as a *French curtain*, she is left free to plot on.

By the way, these curtains so resemble the ladies' dresses and the pelmets which women began constructing over their mushrooming coiffures in the 1770s that, in the first week they went up, Mrs Jervis was amused to find her husband with his head in the newspaper lecturing the window on the state of household expenses and the children's meals!

And . . . the English use the term French to describe things which are so softened that they blend away from being purely straight, square or functional to become dangerously artistic, stylish or elegant. This can apply to anything from a hat to a curtain, a roof, or form of exit ('French leave'), even to a kiss.

The World seen from Three Steps Back

Sensing that self-obsession is no longer a threat, I can look at you without you becoming self-conscious. In fact I would say that you might even be trusted with your own reflection in a mirror. I lead you to the looking-glass. You do not rush up to see yourself, but with restraint stand back first to take in the looking-glass in relation to the console table and its two lights on either side. A very good sign. You *are* . . . ready.

The room is about to perform its magic; a small miracle. If successful, then you will experience a renaissance, or rebirth. For what I call the *Golden Hunch* will rise in your consciousness to take its instinctive place as the template of your higher reasoning. The house has been carefully preparing you and what should happen is what history suggests happened in the minds of those who were part of the sixteenth-century Renaissance. And believe me, if you're smart, you will let it take hold.

Now, before the looking-glass, I ask you to keep *three steps back*. No more, no less. Already, you can see, or sense, that the Space Between is somehow going to be involved. I ask you to close your eyes and find darkness, and then, to open them again, very slowly.

134

I stand back to watch.

'*There. See?*' Before you, or rather behind and all around you, is the glorious reflection of a perfectly balanced eighteenth-century Drawing Room. Again it is like a painting, but this one features *you*. You are its spine; from you everything in your sight begins, just as everything in your sight returns to you. Your own human construction, scale, weight and proportions are the rudiments of all you see. YOU and the Space Between are ONE: so tightly in tune that you both float together in harmony.

I allow you time to soak it all up. You remain captivated, amazed at how the tarnished glass of old Vauxhall plate has actually managed to make you appear as if you really are, already, *in there*.

Renaissance!

I watch you move very slightly to the right – and then to the left – to achieve the most perfect effect. You freeze at what you can see and sense is *just right*: at the very centre. As you close your eyes I whisper, '*Stretch your arms out to both sides. Back in the Renaissance, Leonardo da Vinci had a golden hunch, and in his famous sketch of the Human Proportions he thought aloud. Now, open your eyes and you see it* all.' I ask, '. . . *don't you?*'

An altar in a church

Left-wing   Right-wing

CHAPTER ELEVEN

FOR OUR BODIES TELL US SO

THE GOLDEN HUNCH is:
How *BEST* we *MAY BE* involves the alignment of our existence to the same discipline as that ordained by our own physical form. The symmetry, weight, scale and proportions of our own bodies decree the confines and borders as to where *too much* or *too little* begin and end, and therefore mark right from wrong. This is the root of our reasons *why* and *why not*, and is fixed in our subconscious by the circle and the square. Once *sensed*, its mission is to advise us how to take the most harmonious and least confrontational route in relation to our world and the others of our species. ¶ In one silent

instant the word *taste* is both explained and defined. It is *the regulating instinct we have for adjusting harmony within ourselves, as well as with what exists outside.* It works in the same way that our body does when it asks us to turn down music or add salt or pepper to our food. In any quest to avoid friction the human body is best consulted as our instruction manual, builder's companion, rulebook, atlas and guide. Its finest result comes when taste succeeds in co-ordinating every part of our being to match our best state of physical health; when all is at its tightest, as it is in that reflection before you right now.

When I was nine years old I was taken by my eldest brother to stay with Frank Lloyd Wright's son and wife at Del Mar in California. After two weeks I returned home to be shocked; I couldn't believe the ramshackle ordinariness from which I came. It was not just the Wrights or their house but the whole package, which seemed to fit together and which I noticed only when I'd left it behind. Looking back, it was as if my brother – himself an architect – had plotted the visit for that effect. For sure enough, from that day on, I developed an interest that made me stand three steps back to watch the effect of buildings and places on people's thinking, on their mood and on their behaviour.

This brings us away from the baroque and in the back door of a time within George III's reign, which regarded itself as 'neoclassical'. That is, when the enlightened became so bitten by the idea of a formula for harmony – and a corresponding discipline of logic – that they began to relate more closely to the ancient civilisations than they did to their own native culture.

As we sit here, I manage to persuade you that the commotion you hear outside (a drunken throng of yuppies on their way to Liverpool Street Station) is a herd of goats, pigs and geese being driven past our door on their way to market. I ask you to imagine

how it must have been for European noblemen returning home from the Grand Tour to come face to face with the vulgarity that constituted their own native wealth. Clumsy attempts at symmetry, they could see, were only a beginning.

Sink or Swim

By design, a visitor to this room is swimming in liquid Harmony. I use the term swim for a good reason. We cannot hurt our self when we swim. Football and other sports take place in the air – which is lighter than we are, and the slack provides the space for excess that can result in collision or injury. However, there is no slack between a human and water: we either sink or take to it and swim. The relationship is as tight as it can be, and because we swim to survive, the physique it creates is a natural one.

In the seventeenth century, taste became either too heavy or too plain (Cavalier or Puritan). In the nineteenth century the Victorians would return to heavy taste in a quest to evoke something spiritual which they sensed was wanting. Here in the mid-eighteenth century our minds join with the mid-Georgians in pleasing God, but also in refining taste.

This refining process is, then, *Classical* as opposed to Christian, even if the emphasis on moderation amounts to the same thing. But just as we are still left with Old Isaac's eating parlour downstairs as a reminder of ourselves in another time, so were the mid to late Georgians left to live with the clumsy and grossly expensive monstrosities of baroque taste which – in their minds – they associated with all the legends they knew of senseless wars and outrageous political intrigues, witch-burnings, rampant superstition and mass slaughters.

Starting Where?

And – oh – what a touchy subject is taste! *What is 'just right'? Where does it begin? Where does it end?* And that question that anyone who is unsure of themselves has to ask, *'Who says so?'*

Every Road Led to Rome

Your renaissance was spoonfed; mine was hard work. Both, however, came about in this room. The idea of uneducated me, preaching to my visitors about the age of neoclassicism, the refinement of taste and the Romans, is really absurd! That I do, and that learned people are prepared to listen and accept what I say is, to me, the proof that what is 'Classical' is truly timeless and universal.

I now believe that there is a thread of truth which lies in the air waiting to be intercepted by Man at a point when he is ready for it, and that those who have a natural sensitivity to this are somehow blessed.

I began working on this room one evening in late October 1979. As in the other rooms, I began searching for clues as to what to do. I was not looking for clues to restoration, but more to reincarnation. Working fast, so not to lose the grip on something so fragile as the spiritual thread which was my guide, I waded knee-deep into a colossal task, for this room was a real mess. The panelling had been covered with a thin board, and then wallpapered and more recently painted a pale violet. Literally thousands of nails had to be removed and each hole filled; the box cornice had been removed as had the room's skirting and the chair rail.

£185, four dozen candles, two borrowed tools and a kerbstone outside to employ as sandpaper were really all I had. Abandoned wooden pallets from the market would have to do for timber. Only one week was spent on the kitchen, ten days on the Dining Room; two weeks on the Smoking Room; but this room, I could see, was going to take me into the next year. And what to do? Unlike the other rooms, which were immediately evocative, this one was not. I found three clues to make me think.

The first was that the hearth had been moved over to the centre of the room's main wall. This had both startled and delighted me when I first entered, for I knew from a drawing published in *Stowe's Survey of London* that most neighbouring houses were originally built with their hearths placed over to one side; something which annoyed me intensely. So I went on to read the alteration as an important statement; and indeed, when I removed the thin board which covered the fireplace wall, I realised that it must have been a complicated, costly and filthy affair for whoever originally undertook to carry it out.

The second clue was that someone, some time, went to the trouble of embellishing the three drawing-room windows on the outside of the house with ornamental Chippendale-style fretwork. And while the house's simple early-Georgian façade may be fairly ordinary, this feature is not. Obviously not part of the overall exterior scheme, the applied decoration would appear to be unique. It might show that a new householder had caught on to the idea of *piano nobile*, and wished to emphasise the fact, whereas the previous generation of occupants had not. Or that the windows framed a room containing something rare and highly prized: something treasured. This is the explanation I preferred, which made me want to give the room the best I had. As I worked later into the night something uncanny began to dawn upon me: that I had been collecting the contents for this room from a room I invented in my head when I was eighteen years old.

While working in the eerie darkness of those deserted Spitalfields nights – and with the room and myself working towards the same goal – I have never felt so close to the past. My mind travelled in a way that structured and made better sense of things I already knew. It was as if I was working alongside Time, and with no company and no modern equipment aboard. I even found myself asking, *'What would they (the Georgians) do now?'* – instead of *'What does everybody do when . . . ?'* Soon I realised that the third clue was, quite naturally, being taken from my own Golden Hunch. What to do, and what not to do in putting back what was missing (and with the fear of architectural historians nosing about and lifting their hands in the air to cry out: *'Wrong! Wrong!'*), I had to look at myself in order to make up something that, in human terms, *looked so right* that it had to be right.

Architecture:
A formal temple-fronted façade
Sculpture:
Canova's "The Three Graces"

Music:
Amadeus ("God's love") Mozart

Humour:
*"The actress
to the bishop"*
Sport:
*A game called
Tennis*
Dance:
The Minuet
Society:
A bow to a curtsey
"Majority Rule":
The "United" States of America

A King:
The "United" Kingdom

Invisible or marked – all about *three*:
the CENTRE cradling the Harmony
worthy as a seat for GOD.

143

I worked as late into the night as my candles and my firewood lasted, sometimes even into the early hours of the next morning. Friends would occasionally turn up after eating a curry in Brick Lane or would come in from a concert and keep me company as I worked. They seemed intrigued to watch, and I heard that someone who had seen me remove my socks and soak them in the wet plaster, in order to fill in and then mould into shape a missing piece of cornice, was now going around town describing No. 18 as 'restoration comedy'. I can remember how, with my hunger and tiredness, once they had gone, parts of their conversation continued to go round and round in my head.

One such conversation was over the alteration – or repositioning – of the hearth, which seemed to my visitors to make the room's proportions come together to appear *stately*. How can it be, I found myself wondering, that a room so small might be described as stately, while so much larger ones – rambling and more richly decorated – are not? If only I owned a dictionary, I thought. (Something, no doubt, you've been thinking all along.)

In the night I remembered hearing somewhere that the Latin for hearth is *focus*. By the morning I found myself rummaging through stacks of used timber and my collection of wood carvings, plaster and composition mouldings in order to construct a chimneypiece to mark – indeed to celebrate – the centre. I knew that my initiative in doing so was related to what made explorers and generals pitch their flags on the land they found or conquered. Alive within me was the feeling that made the Ancients build their temples and place the images of their gods at the centre. It struck me, too, *why* the Georgians not only centred their hearths, but also designed and embellished their famous chimneypieces, as they did their door cases: to stand as miniature Classical temples. Bull's-eye!

Dennis Severs had grabbed the Romans, the Renaissance and the neoclassical movement – by the balls.

Bull's-Eye!

So having marked the centre, I went on to finish and decorate this room as an exercise in harmony. Any barrier separating one side from the other was removed so that both bowed with grateful homage to the chimneypiece at the centre: a temple to celebrate a union, not a wall to underline a seam. From there, with nothing too much, nothing too little – the space between things regulated to be just right. Now all I had to do was to take the same structure inside my head.

CHAPTER TWELVE

A JOURNEY TO THE CENTRE OF TASTE

'Look at him,' I say, directing your attention to the right of the door where a copy of a Roman bust sits high up atop an imposing gilt bracket. You look up. *'Edward Jervis makes that man his children's hero. Oh, not for any great deed and certainly not for his good looks or what they might see of an elaborate robe; but rather for a godlike aura.'* After a just-right pause, I continue, *'You see, the Roman has hit the centre mark: he's . . . there! risen to such height that he sees the whole picture, and the impact of his resolve has driven itself inward, right to his core. Now it radiates outward giving him a look, a kind of godlike trance. Perfect repose — see? It's a kind of three steps back expression: one that says "nobody's fault".'*

This always gives me considerable pleasure to impart, for it touches upon something that most visitors are aware of and yet have never actually heard anyone define. I am speaking of the aura of confidence and inner peace that we sense in others, regardless of age or physical appearance. To catch perfect repose is the ultimate test of any sculptor's ability, for though much will change with fashion and time, this aura which radiates *inside out* will remain classic, it is the closest we can align Man to God. It may be that its lack of recognition by our own time makes modern sculpture disguise itself by going abstract, or by camouflaging itself under 'style'.

'Edward Jervis', I wish you to know, *'hopes that by his fatherly instruction this look will grace the faces of his children. He knows that their view of things must be taken in from the centre; that only by reaching deep and lifting them high can he help them stand the tests of age and Time.'*

Sitting side by side we can sense the room balancing its symmetry around us. The scene locks together to balance on a ball. Holding my hand in the air, I explain how a musician might strike up and keep playing a solid single tone in order to mark the peace between us; an orator might call for silence. Buddha, I explain, would call this state *the middle way* and readers of graphs and statistics might show us its proof in what they call the *bell-shaped curve*. A painter must arrange things to and from a *vanishing point*, while an architect might mark it with a temple-fronted façade, like that on the National Gallery, the White House, or any older public building.

The room's symmetry asks a visitor to know the strength of their right hand, as well as the gentle and modifying ability of their left hand, and to remember that they are asked to lift the right hand in taking an oath.

'Now, why is it that the Jervises might be assumed to be nervous of the "cock-eyed" or "long-faced"; of snakes and reptiles, other people's children, a certain type of politics and . . . modern jazz?'

The Jervis Family motto is
'God the centre; not the end'.

When our couple share this fire alone an instinct appears to make Mrs Jervis harbour protection of the corner to the left of the fire. As the holder of the egg – and with the softer complexion – she keeps a 'pole screen' and fan at her side to protect her from the direct heat. The corner is also equipped with a silver kettle for the administration of sustenance and hospitality, and a sewing basket to contain her 'work'. The chemical sign for women is: [♀], or copper: her strength is that she is pliable.

The chemical sign for men is: [♂] or iron, and Mr Jervis, being the host of the seed, strides forth to the chair to the right of the hearth. There, nearer to the cold draughts and the dangers of the street, he keeps his sword; and with command of the room's only door, his right hand is in the correct position for combat if anyone should attack his wife or the nest. On the open road he will keep to the left of any oncoming stranger for that same reason. Neither side would offend the balance by sitting so close to the fire that they block the heat.

– On Earth as it is in Heaven –

The framed decorations around the windows of this room advertise that something rare is contained within. It is the formula for Harmony which each visitor carries in with them, and which the room seeks to draw out. I often see it in a departing visitor's face.

Amen.

INCIDENT... INCIDENT... INCIDENT...

Dear Visitor; there has been an incident.

A teacup has fallen to the floor, where it lies broken; a bowl filled with lumps of sugar has been spilled across the tea table and the children's house of cards has collapsed; and all in the very instant of *Nirvana!*

Be warned, there is a child aboard: a Miss Sophie Jervis. All this is her mischief. Virtually illiterate, she has little or no interest in her parents' Classical thinking, finer tastes or higher ideals. It has long been suspected that the midget interrupts *by design*.

She is responsible – you should know – for the excavation in the floor of the cellar, where she will persist in being fascinated by the low, mud-hut, cave-dwelling culture of her native homeland instead of the noble civilisation that was once Rome! A particular problem in our own case is that it is she who bears the chamber-stick which conveys us on, with light, forwards in time.

The child's timing is a well-observed and particularly infuriating part of her mischief-making. Always spot-on, she appears when things are either nearing perfection, or else at their very worst. The child . . . *gets in the way.*

Miss Sophie J. is best kept outside on the stairs and landings; notices are pasted to the doors at keyhole height which read: 'Private': so . . . be careful. The silly little thing will sometimes slip into the room without being seen. Not 'Classical' but round, she *rolls* with Time.

As the door glides open I pinch the shoulder of your jacket to lift you to attention. Into the Drawing Room enters the first procession: three female refugees led by their hostess, Elizabeth Jervis. Up the stairs they have travelled, to withdraw from the cockpit of pitched differences and clouds of tobacco smoke still festering below. We close our eyes and hold our noses as the hostess and the other ladies offload the secrets of their sex and drain their bladders, 'fuss before the glass' – as Mr Jervis puts it – and then freshen their faces, arrange and powder their hair. When we open our eyes the evidence of this has been removed and the tea table erected and made ready with refreshments. On one side, water boils over a spirit lamp in an elaborate silver kettle on a stand. Other details suggest that amusements such as cards and music are in store. All is prepared for the arrival of the men, who, if they are still speaking to one another and able to climb the stairs, will sooner or later bow to a natural instinct to join with the opposite sex.

High Life

If classic means timeless and universal, then it must be right: nothing too much nor too little, nothing unbalanced. Up here protective wool and real hair are discarded and our company will appear well-shaven, smooth, polished – wearing silks and satins trimmed with gold and seed lustrings. White hose and richly buckled shoes are their base and powdered wigs their capitals. Up here they will not use the clumsy tin-glazed delft pottery we saw below, but the finest eggshell-thin Oriental porcelain, or English attempts at the same manufactured in 'hard paste'. The more non-porous and the purer the white, the better and the more expensive. Up here, even sugar and bread are refined to be pure white.

CHAPTER THIRTEEN

A BALANCING ACT

In this house – a visitor without imagination can be dangerous in the same way that they might be in a kitchen or in bed: in politics such people are lethal. However, more dangerous are those with unstructured imaginations who will employ fancy to imagine absolutely anything, and often make themselves the centre. That simply will not do and those seen 'glorying' here have also been seen tumbling down its stairs. Now that our thoughts are aligned to the same template as our bodies, and our imaginations bonded in harmony, what we imagine here should be just right; we can have a little fun.

Tick – TASTE – Tock

I look about the room to say with childlike enthusiasm: *'See? Everything is standing at attention! – Someone's coming.'* I become an actor of the Silent Screen, placing Mrs Jervis's chair before her tea table. You watch me imagine the servants (some hired), dressed in their finest livery, taking up their positions within the room, on the landing and down in the hall. Suddenly the 'At Home' invitations, displayed across British upper-crust chimneypieces, should make sense; for only when all this is done, and the stage is fully set, can the footman announce to a caller that his mistress is indeed 'At Home'.

In medieval times – during troubles – fire covers or *curfews* were ordered over the fires in cities and towns so that the poor had no other alternative but to take their troubles to bed.

The candles are all lit. Lights cost money and so only the rich could once afford to penetrate the night. From the creaks and whispers we hear out on the stairs we are to know that Mrs Jervis has allowed her children to stay awake past their bedtime to view the Drawing Room and the first Landing fully lit. It is a rare sight for their little eyes – like that of a fully lit and decorated Christmas tree for Victorian children a century later. The children are positioned up on the next bend in the stairs so that they can look down to see the guests parade up the stairs.

Mrs Edward Jervis's Court is most certainly not to be imagined like that of Henry VIII, with guests holding venison bones up to their greasy red faces. Ruddy Rebecca and the kitchen are in the basement; the Dining Room for the low pursuit of eating is down on the 'ground floor', and up here things associated with a preoccupation for survival, like hunger itself, are purposely kept at bay. Instead little nibbles – refreshments, canapés, appetisers, tea biscuits and 'petits fours' – will keep any hint of gluttony from getting in the way of higher matters. And if – during your game of cards – you really cannot fight off your hunger, then the footman might ask Rebecca to cut slices of cold meats left over from luncheon and sandwich them together between two pieces of bread to serve you as a social snack: as Lord Sandwich prefers. And – so far up from the kitchen as we are – 'toast' will be served cold, with no rough edges: you can imagine the crusts removed first.

Now – a Withdrawing Room is no more a 'sitting room' for sitting, than it is a 'lounge' for lounging. It is society's formal stage. Making yourself too comfortable might suggest a kickback to old-fashioned individualism. The furniture does not face the fire but towards stage-centre, so that the guests can 'circle' while not getting anchored to one another or too confined to one corner.

At Court only the king may sit, and his master of ceremonies decides which of his courtiers deserves a chair. *Up here* that will be decided by our hostess – sharing the mental conditioning which gave the nation its seemingly innate sense of hierarchy. Even when entering the humblest cottage an immediate assessment had to be made as to who, in terms of seniority of age or rank, should sit nearest to the heat.

Our chairs here are social and are therefore embellished at the front, but not at the back; for they live up against the wall and face the space between. The 'chair rail', the 'dado' between the pedestal and the column of the panelling, protects the wall's paint from the chair backs, and a chair's back legs will often extend gracefully outward at the base to serve that same purpose. Until recently many of an older generation pulled their chairs out and away from the wall before being seated.

'But . . . where is she?'

The room suggests that Mr and Mrs Jervis should be imagined in the *Doric Order*, to remain invisibly in harmony with the room. Neither are grand or lofty enough to stick out as *Corinthian* (like Mrs Jervis's Tory grandmother), nor are they stocky or sturdy enough (neither have served in the army) to be *Tuscan*. Certainly they are not willowy, feminine or chic enough to be *Ionic*. So yes, by looking about us and recalling the uses of the classical orders in Western architecture, *Doric* is just right.

Our couple do not share the sturdy legs of Rebecca's chair in the kitchen, nor the pigeon-toed 'Braganza foot' of Old Isaac's high-backs. *Up here* Mrs Jervis will be camouflaged from the eyes of any non-believer by standing, like her chairs, with her feet pointing more elegantly outwards. Dignified, confident and graceful, this position suggests a more relaxed formality as well as a generosity of spirit.

'Ten minutes to two,' Mrs Jervis will often shout to her children and servants when an important guest is being conducted up from the hall. This was an image most people had of the well-heeled: the right foot forward before the left, heels touching and the toes pointing away from each other. Mrs Jervis, her husband and grandmother, whose faces are also here in the room with us, must, like all other portrait sitters, have their feet in this position to effect the elegant posture we see them painted in.

'Well-heeled' is supposed to be derived from the red heels worn at the Court of Louis XIV, who had so fine a dancing foot – and legs – that he liked to display them to their best advantage. Thus the 'first position', or the position from which all others begin. The king's posture, like a good chair, thus appeared in the way that was its most elegant and imposing.

Today a person's image is still fashioned upwards, by the position of their feet. The whole world laughed and cried to watch a poor tramp from south London, Charlie Chaplin, with a bowler hat and umbrella, arranging his feet to stand like a gentleman.

Something has caught your eye. The flicker and the shadows created by the artificial light has suddenly brought Mrs Jervis more closely into view. I draw your attention to the room's relief carvings and to its wall brackets and sconces coated with gold leaf, catching the candlelight like the caps of waves do the sun in evening light. The taste for gilding ornament came with the same experience of candlelight, as did the use of jewellery, silks of different textures and colours, with sea-pearls and sequins. All with the same eye-dazzling and flattering effect.

I point to the domed, cylinder shape of the cup which sits upside-down before us on the tea table: *'... the outline of her skirts, the same combination of the rectangle and the square. If you touch one of these pieces*

of silk . . . here!', I say, taking your hand to a curtain, *'you will find it to be almost like paper in its texture, a quality little known to us today.'* And looking over your shoulder, I add, *'You will know, if you should hear it rustle, that Mrs Jervis is somewhere . . . very nearby.'*

I begin to circle the tea table, speak, and occasionally break out into a figure-of-eight to encircle you – too.

'Anything employed by a hostess in the art of tea-drinking is of the most delicate, sometimes almost toy-like, manufacture. It is often done to confuse our hostess's skin with her tea dishes.' Gesturing at the nest of Lowestoft tea dishes before us, I point out that within the painted decoration on each dish there is a tiny amount of the very same red blush that she uses. *'Her porcelain complexion – so white – differs so much from that of her cook, that Rebecca and the other servants have decided amongst themselves (from what they see of their mistress's wrists) that the age-old rumour is true: that higher classes do indeed have "blue blood".'*

Our Own 'Conversation'

What is being pieced together in our minds here is a scene by which eighteenth-century society might be familiar to us: a form of painting called the 'conversation picture'. These normally feature family or club members who are 'captured' busy at something; they are placed in a setting, either real or invented, just like this one. But instead of a camera lens catching people in mid-motion, an eighteenth-century painter would be paid to capture a group frozen into formal postures, sometimes Classical, as the Ancients were familiar to them only in statue form. The expressions and postures of the sitters will therefore appear stuffed – and they rarely come across as likeable.

Unlike people in the seventeenth century, who might like to see themselves painted in theatrical poses to instil an element of awe, and unlike the coming generation, who would attempt to warm things up with sentiment, the cold looks of this generation are the faces of those fashioned by Reason alone. However, to the neoclassical mind, itself so fascinated by excavation, this was how they wished to be caught: frozen, smart and joining ranks with the Ancients in waiting for rediscovery.

Imagine *precisely* that: *Charles Townley's Library in Park Street* (posed sketching amongst his own collection of antiquities), by Johann Zoffany.

And now, *The Crewe Conversation* (a large family gathering, at tea), by Arthur Devis.

And now imagine this, *The Jervis Conversation* (interrupted during an assembly in their London Drawing Room, while at tea and cards), by, of course, You and Me.

The question induced by each is, *'And just what's been going on here – then?'* Hence, the 'conversation piece'.

So, in order for it to be right, those whom we imagine here will have to be busy: at tea, at cards, 'botanising', reading a book; their son William having only just shot into the room from flying a kite – animated, but never idle. At the same time they should be arranged in balance so that they will stand up in Time, like statues, and not fall over to one side.

Music for the Thaw

Tick – TASTE – *tock, tick* – TASTE – *tock, tick* – TASTE – *tock* . . .

My silence lets you hear the gentle tock of the clock. Then, to the same rhythm, we begin to hear music.

'*Liquid architecture,*' I say looking into the space. '*Music will make any square begin to roll. Now, just watch our hostess begin to thaw: send her out on her morning ride to a "Canto"; have a tiff with Mr Jervis to a "Scherzo", see them make up to an "Adagio"; scold the children to a "Galliard", strut to a "Pavane", and chase Rebecca around the kitchen table with a broom – of course – to a "Rondo".*'

What we are hearing is the Hornpipe Minuet from Handel's *Water Music* suite. Just right, *tick* – TASTE – *tock*, it makes one side of the room bow to the other while it teases with the space between. And with Mrs Jervis by now so perfectly placed, the great thaw can begin.

Into the Looking-Glass – and In for the Swim

Tick – TASTE – *tock. In three–four time. Tick* – TASTE – *tock.*
In three–four time.

Suddenly we hear the rustle of silk. I reach over and spin you round to face the mirror, positioning you three steps back; you know what to do. Outside we hear coaches drawing up at the door while names are being announced – shouted – up the stairs. Behind us the room fills with the clinking of teacups, glasses and the harmonious voices of society. Things begin to sparkle as we hear women joined by men and bass joined by treble: the picture is *whole*! As you close our eyes to see – *spin* – *spin* – *spin* – they open again and swishhh . . . *in between* we go. *There*, or rather – *here*, we are. Now, you'll either see it . . . or you won't.

The Jervis Conversation
by You and Me

Leonardo's sketch and the Golden Hunch become our atlas and our guide.

The heavy stucco ceiling above us begins with the same *rectangular* form that dominates the rest of the room, until somehow it develops into the opposite: at the very centre, the *circle*. Beneath we watch our hostess at work to achieve the same effect, to make round what Man's world insists on making square. Such is the classic task of any host, any time, anywhere.

Mrs Jervis is doing her best, and has helped to ease the room's formality by introducing a new and very fashionable *circular* tea table. Thus, she and her guests might feel more at ease with one another than they would if the tea ritual were still conducted at a rectangular table with herself seated at the top, as it was in her youth. A 'meeting' is *square* – with someone at the top to lead, whereas surely a 'party' is *round*. Chairs are now brought forward to form a circle, and from the tea table her guests may pivot to *circulate* and *make the rounds*.

Looking across to the other looking-glass, this one Palladian, you will see Edward Jervis. Or a mirror that looks just like him. It, too, is tailored in mahogany with gold accessories, and he shares a waistcoat of exactly the same outline and cut. Even his wig, with no centre parting, is of the same design as the room and everything in it; his wig is crowned with a dome, and has two neatly rolled curls attending each side.

At Tea in the Space Between
by You and Me

Tick – TASTE – *tock, tick* – TASTE – *tock,*
and still in three–four time.

You sit intrigued to watch Mrs Jervis go about such an unashamedly feminine task. She first unlocks her tea caddy to bring out a quantity of leaves. Then, after checking that they are suitably crushed, she mixes a small morsel of her blend, for which she has already organised the heating of the water. Now she warms the pot and each

dish before pouring the tea. A perforated 'moat spoon' is used to
moat off leaves that still float upon the top. This has its own spoon
tray, and we see her insert the spear end of its handle down into the
teapot spout to keep clear the passage of loose leaves. I notice that
we are both watching this as some might a High Church Mass, and
that at any social snag, something tactless or spilled, we are amused
to see how she will immediately pull her guests' attention back to the
subject that unites them all: to tea.

167

At Cards in the Space Between
by You and Me

Tick – TASTE – tock; tick – TASTE – tock;
and still in perfect three– four time.

The tea table is now cleared, dismantled and then removed so that the card table can be erected. Around it we see some gather to stand in a circle, while others are seated to play. I lean over to you and whisper: *'Remember the smoke stream? . . . Well, just watch all this. The instinct to hunt and kill, developed into warfare and then to sport, has now arrived up here in the Drawing Room, but as a ritual squared up to be a table-based game of flirtation. The same low strategies, ploys, even the scheming, are made subtle and gentle, but they are still the same.'*

I go quiet so that we feel the mood as we peer over the shoulders of the other guests into the candle-lit arena of the card game. With the room so darkened our Protestants of both sexes can feel more at ease to play and sip sweet wines. Money is *low*, so their bets are made with 'counters' instead, carved of ivory or mother-of-pearl; we see them glow and shimmer. Not a word is spoken as cat-like intrigues begin: subtle observations and carefully guarded side glances, all flashing so perfectly to the firelight from behind. Our conversation picture now becomes one of the elaborate silhouettes of the same period.

I whisper of it, *'Hear? All those expressions we know:* "Not worth the candle"' – meaning the game is a bad one. She's 'a card'. Hear? Some would say she's had a 'raw deal' – but always 'plays her cards well'. So well, that one might suspect she has something 'up her sleeve'. Nothing too 'under-hand', she's only 'playing a round'. Soon she will have to 'put her cards on the table'. I add that a good game, conducted fairly, is 'a good deal'.

The 'Sandwich'
She's 'a Card'
A 'Raw Deal'
'Plays Her Cards Well'
'Something up Her Sleeve'
It's 'On the Cards'
'. . . Not Worth the Candle'

Again we go silent. Tick – TASTE – tock, and sure enough – we now begin to hear a request for pardon; of course someone has missed the mark and is taken over to one side. We hear someone speak of his 'level best' and refer to the 'straight and narrow'. We may have to use the French word *gauche* (left) for the one who goes at it all the wrong way around. To any contribution – performed, said, sung, read or acted – instinct will make us clap our hands; and if it is exceedingly good, something seems to ask us to stand up to add strength to our ovation. Something related to the spine has triumphed. Not because of manners, nor because of etiquette, but because our bodies tell us so.

The Rude Awakening

Tick – TASTE – Tock – you seem to have drifted off to sleep. It is time to misquote Madonna, *ladies – without attitude; fellahs – in gentlest of moods; a timeless pose – Huh! . . . quickly: VESUVIUS! – So let's go! – and let's get to it . . . VOGUE!'*

– And I clap my hands – **POP!** Like a swan, Mrs Jervis turns her head, while Mr Jervis places one hand in his waistcoat to return into

perfect repose. William moves to the foreground to tend to his house of cards as the female guests, an Ionic Three Graces, lock arms to gaze off in three different directions. Our bodies instruct the men to do the same, and at the very centre Mrs Jervis's grandmother, Lady St John ('Corinthian'), rises aloft from behind. But, **POP!**

Lady St John is suddenly a chimneypiece, Edward Jervis a looking-glass, and his wife – only a chair. But – there it is in our minds: *the Jervis Conversation.* Interrupted but frozen in our memories. We both applaud until something makes us feel we should stand. I lean over to say, *'And, just what's been happening here – then?'*

Tick – (TASTE) – Tock

When Lights Are Low

Although the other guests have drifted off and out into the night, we remain behind. Still seated, frozen. Outside we hear servants shouting 'Chair ho!' – or 'Chairs home', so that the waiting sedan may be lifted and carried forth to our doors. Indoors the lights have all burned so low that we can see the red and orange light of the hand-held flares outside, behind the blinds. 'Linkboys' carrying torches are coming forth to offer light, protection and advice on the state of roads and the safest routes home. 'Tips' are being negotiated – _T_o _I_nsure _P_rompt _S_ervice. And so we join our fine pair of hosts in calling out from their door, *'Chair home!'*

The candles around us are now burning so low to the silver, gilt, crystal or brass of their holders that the light they cast reflects differently from the dazzling light we have grown used to. The lines and boundaries between things begin to blur before our eyes. As the picture mellows, the atmosphere seems more relaxed; some would say it becomes more natural, while others would see it as a slide backwards – away from Reason and to mystery.

'Cheerio!'

Our Sin

In the distance a thunderclap cracks and rolls. You jolt. *'Look,'* I say, nodding into the dark at something that sparkles, *'on the tea table Mrs Jervis has left her silver patch box behind. Hallmarked silver – and so very small . . . Visitor, why not take it?'* I cup my mouth in one hand to whisper, *'No one is looking; go on – put it in your pocket as a souvenir of tonight's adventure. Surely no one will notice if the smallest thing in the room – for which there is no pair – goes missing?'*

Or will they? The Mrs Jervis we have created will sense that something is off-balance even before she identifies what it is that is missing. The arrangement on her tea table, and with it the room that hosts it, are no longer at peace. You will have stolen, and internally you too will no longer balance. *Boom, boom, boom,* your pulse quickens, blood pressure rises, nerves may make you sweat; there is a desire to smoke or – dare I say it – even chew gum. Guilt will, with time, begin to rearrange and harden your features to appear defensive. You – visitor, only recently so perfectly structured to balance – are about to become a mess. If Rebecca's cat were perched upon your knee right now, she would sense at once that you have departed from your former state of grace and no longer qualify to be trusted with her weight: she will move off. If questioned, you may collapse and confess your guilt – or you will lie.

You have paid for your trinket with a loss of harmony within yourself and with the outside world. The space between will become uncomfortable when others are forced to take sides or to play dumb. The wrong person may get the blame and the balance will begin to fracture.

Boom-boom, boom-boom, boom-boom . . .

Without a word I open the box and lay the note before you for your inspection.

'From Harmony you have stolen: watch what happens to you now.'

We sneak out on to the dark landing, where we find ourselves within earshot of two voices. Again, one is heard through the door of the Smoking Room. It is young William Jervis – to his father: the voice of a coming generation.

'Father, if there be a God, then surely He is the God of Nature too, and not just Man alone! Is it not the arrogance of Man that makes him think himself the "crown of creation": that everything should be made to balance in the symmetry of his own form? There are no straight lines and no squares in Nature, Father.' On hearing this I think, and then point up to the florid rococo ceiling above us. True: it must be *in the air* – that there are no squares, and no straight lines in Nature.

In the Dark

Reason insists on *light, sight* and a *higher view*, it fears darkness for obstructing its path. This is why the picture that Reason will paint is so often flat: we look forwards only at what sits before the eye. Deprived of light, we might easily revert to using instincts and even fall prey to superstition. That much, by now, we know. Look what has happened. With lights so low, our imaginations are already beginning to take liberties. Our couple's children have awakened to invade and play havoc with our perfect world. Reason is nervous of children. Look – see? The banished Miss Sophie J. has arrived and is busy at her work. Reason shudders to think what might happen, in the dark.

PART THREE

Up and Down
— This House
and Your Heart

CHAPTER FOURTEEN

TWO SIDES TO EVERYTHING, NO SIDE FORWARD

Heaven-on-Earth is a hard act to follow. Some believe that upon reaching the state of perfection there is nothing else to do but either go down into the grave or up to Heaven: to die. Most of us say to the possibility of Heaven or Hell, *'Not yet.'* ¶ Phew! And do you realise that we did all that downstairs – *horizontally?* From the minute we left the kitchen our imaginations have been at work in the two-sided symmetry of our own bodies, trying to balance and perfect a peace between sides. Come to think of it, everything produced by reason – architecture, cars, boats and trains, politics, manners and music – they all must balance horizontally like the aeroplane, if they are to succeed in moving forward.

The trouble is, that having found the perfect state in the Drawing Room, you would have quite happily sat in that chair and slept right through the rest of the night. Back and forth – tick-tock – '*square*', '*flat*' or '*hum-drum*' – the outcome of balancing out frictions so that any pair of *pros* and *cons* are in complete harmony can be a '*stick-in-the-mud*' – Deadlock. Rebecca often says of what she hears in the Drawing Room: '*Two sides to everything, no side forward.*' flipping a coin is more decisive than the phrase, '*But on the other hand, there is always the other argument that states . . .*' (Someone made a T-shirt in the 1970s: '*I used to be indecisive, but now I'm not sure.*')

As you, like others, fell asleep in the Drawing Room, I remember thinking to myself that the only thing that night I could do to keep you awake would be either to introduce someone *High* – like a Prince – or someone *Low* – like a dangerous criminal. You see, though we may reason *back and forth*, we feel *high or low*. *Boom-boom, boom-boom* – it is only what excites the heart that will speed a mind out of deadlock. So our bodies tell us.

So where to go? Time to move on emotionally: *UP and DOWN*. Again we climb, this time, in a hush, to the Second Landing.

We halt at the bend in the stairs to receive an unexpected surprise. It is a smell; and before us on a little tripod table in the corner sits a vase of newly cut flowers – stocks. Their freshness of colour and fragrance make a powerful impression upon our senses: enough to make us realise that so far the whole picture has been created *by* Man, *for* Man. Nature we left below.

By now we know light to be our lure. But in looking ahead we are surprised to see not light, but darkness brooding, almost like an

approaching storm – the clock mounted high upon the wall ahead of us suddenly startles us to crank and strike the half-hour. *Ding-dong! Ding-dong!* – its rhythm our minds decree is a fraction too fast to match our heartbeats! Not *just right*. The effort of climbing the stairs means that our own heartbeats are also a little too aroused.

Ah! Sophie's chamber-stick rests on the floor before the door to our next destination. I use its meagre flame to expose the walls, which are decorated in *découpage*, or hand-cut paper, thus creating here what some might recognise as a 'print room'.

I whisper that it was apparently the children who engaged in a little fun by decorating the walls and ceilings with old printed portraits, many of whom are the faces of Edward Jervis's clients published in the *European Magazine*. Each print was crowned with one of the royal coat of arms cut from a newspaper. Black paper borders were then cut from what seem to be the lines of an old printed Act of Parliament, and the whole confection was pasted up in framed patterns on to panelled walls, which were painted, or became with age, a murky grey. The ceiling above us, with grotesque masks and bullfrogs, is modelled by hand in *papier mâché*. Though it is all rather gloomy, somehow it is still a surprising delight: what might be called a 'findersplease'.

I watch you bend forward to look more closely, in a manner which suggests that you are not critical, but impressed and charmed by what you see. Though I have watched you stiffen and then loosen up in refining yourself, you have certainly never bent forward to look at anything before. Is curiosity turning into inspiration? As I watch you narrow your eyes to examine – *up and down* – each of the decorated panels, a piece of music drifts in from the distance and you lift your head to listen. It is religious, and more emotional in its appeal than the symmetry of the hornpipe which made our heads move from *side to side* – like a metronome. This piece begs your emotions to join in with it and 'harmonise'.

'Découpage' – so I explain – 'is the art of the poor, and the fact that it has been constructed in so amateur a fashion is what makes it so charming, especially compared to the professional taste and quality we have recently become used to. And more, that its decoration runs up and down is such a surprise. Everything on the piano nobile *balanced back and forth; whereas up here it does so up and down. For all this is conceived in the "Gothic" taste.'*

SHOCK! Boom-boom, boom-boom, boom-boom. SHOCK!

'*Gothic!* In *this* house!' Your expression changes with mine. First the art of the poor, and now *Gothic?* The submissive lunacy which once had man bypass his own ability to reason and point up to beg and cry to God for every answer. '*How can the Jervises, Protestants, let themselves slide from Classical perfection into the dark superstition of Gothic ignorance?*' As your heart races, I interpret this from your expression and say aloud, '*Lord bless me*', on your behalf.

I quickly explain that history is no straight line, and that fashionable taste may have returned to 'Gothic' as a style, due to an *emotional* wanting, or craving. A need for mystery, romance and spirituality, so much a part of a human life, but which Reason alone cannot see and therefore will not allow a space for.

Still recovering from the shock, you breathe in and stiffen *up* and arch your feet in order to dig them *down*. Oh dear, you really do *feel* high or low!

Up or Down

People say of skyscrapers, '*God only knows why we build these things!*' God does. A mind will explain – to death – the theory on economy of space, whereas a heart will tell us straight that tall buildings excite us to see, to design, to build; they impress and test us. Great height, like the Empire State Building, and great lows – like the Grand Canyon – can often take our breath away. (Excuse the use of two American examples, but what impresses foreigners like myself about England is that nothing is . . . *breathtaking*; and if it tries to be, it comes across as unnatural. It is natural that mildness, as in climate

'Classical' remains determined to be 'just right'.

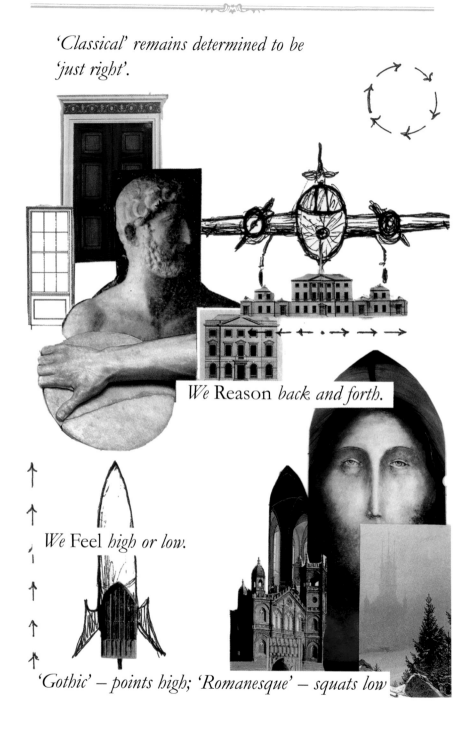

We Reason *back and forth.*

We Feel *high or low.*

'Gothic' – *points high;* 'Romanesque' – *squats low*

184

and terrain, makes things tone themselves down so that they have to come together to be rich and impressive as a whole.)

Reason in terms of architecture is the aeroplane, the White House and Buckingham Palace, just as in musical terms it would translate into Classical counterpoint. By contrast, a rocket is breathtaking, in that it is designed solely for the vertical direction, with no wings; it is the spire of Salisbury Cathedral or a Gregorian chant. A Gothic horror story could only be set in an *up and down* romantic affair with gables, chimneys and towers; overgrown from the ground below, with lightning flashing in the sky *above*.

Advance Warning

On the second floor I expect you either to fight its romance, on the grounds that it will conflict with your recently sharpened sense of practical Reason, or else – as better suits some – you may instantly become more relaxed on being asked to think from the heart. However, the conflict is with yourself; for Reason and Passion, without God at the Centre, are oil and water. You might well imagine the frustration a heart might feel if you were to pause in the middle of telling a neighbour about a murder on his doorstep in order to explain the origins of all the words you were using. This conflict between Reason and Passion is the basic formula at the core of every human struggle between any younger and older generation; between Edward Jervis – a low dissenter, and his wife – a high Anglican. It is the conflict between *what we understand we must do, and what we feel we want to do.*

East Enders refer to middle-class thinkers who can only act on what they see as *wankers.*

So, Up or Down?

Did anyone actually tell us that God is *way up high* and that Satan lives *way down low*? Or did we instinctively know that our place is at the *CENTRE* where we were born and were designed to belong? A microscope can now prove that going small can go on for ever and ever, a telescope can take us out into the universe, for ever and ever. So – deadlock, and 'God', the keystone translated into passion, is 'love'. Neither too high, nor in lust too low, but the subtle warmth that is *Love-Constant*, is.

From there – we can look down to recognise that it is a low passion related to hate that leads to war and destruction. *Down low* exist all those deep-rooted things that we love so much that we hate those who threaten them. Our roots, clan or tribe, gang or race, family, nation or language – without love all become hostile and territorial. By looking *up* we find our godlier ideals; but again, our love for these higher tastes can clash with those who see God differently, and again we may fight. *Nationalism* is *low*: its root is hate, in that it needs an enemy; *patriotism* is *high*, its root is love of country. In architecture churches or civic buildings sometimes start with a square foundation, but can sometimes end in a dome; never the other way around.

To the Ancient Greeks the downwards pull was in response to the call of the God Dionysus (the Roman Bacchus) – the likeable God of wine with his revelry and hedonism. Fall down with him and you will frolic; he offers merriment and fun – but like Rebecca, he offers no higher view and greater plan. The pull *upward* is the one towards art, enlightenment and beauty. Cooler, its God is Apollo.

The horizontal and vertical lines join together in Leonardo's sketch to agree on one thing: that it is wise to draw together and not to venture out too far in any direction of darkness, even for the sake of a short-term thrill. For evil, represented by the Devil, has a final card to play: it *turns on and destroys* those who befriend it, like a gangster in an old movie.

CHAPTER FIFTEEN

PASSIONS BEGIN AT HOME

Imagine – carved upon the front exterior of Bath Abbey: Christians on ladders to Heaven. ¶ And here they are – rioting again! The excavation down in the cellar, along with the Gothic confection up here on the landing, might suggest that children are getting a little restless. Perhaps they sense that such civilised things as exist in the Drawing Room are sometimes without warmth? The architecture of Rome, German music, French food and wine, not to mention all those Italian fashions and pasta, have clearly nothing much to do with the world they see from their nursery windows. To them, the objects on the *piano nobile* rest on top of the soil, but are not rooted. What they feel is that the *real* England, gnarled and crooked as it may be, is hiding high and low, waiting for all alien things to blow back to whence they came.

Mr Jervis is always puzzled, when he and his wife decide on neoclassical Osterley Park or Syon House for an outing, by the way that the children will root for Horace Walpole's Gothic mad-house at Strawberry Hill, Twickenham. How they make the coach lurch by rushing to the same window to view any old, burnt-out ruin, or wander into the city's ancient lanes, which their parents refer to as 'shambles'. Any tall structure makes them want to scale it to look out from its top. *Boom-boom, boom-boom, boom-boom* – their little hearts speed up as they set out to explore things *which cannot be explained*. Too often their parents notice that any question which Reason alone cannot answer, is never laid aside, but asked again and again.

Talking of which . . . have you noticed that, even with all that banter in the spirit of 'neoclassicism', there's nothing of that description in the house? The rooms have a kind of old-fashioned 'merchant baroque' charm – like those of Christopher Wren's time; something Edward Jervis remembered from his youth and wanted for himself when one day he became successful. It suggests too that our couple, like many in their day, appreciate and embrace imported Classicism, but only to the extent that fits the tastes they have for the things of their own native homeland. They prefer things with roots and not what lies only on the surface.

During their stay in Bath each autumn, the children are sent off to do drawings of the noble architecture of Queen's Square (the rectangle) and the Circus (the circle), yet they return with sketches of that ugly old eyesore, the Gothic Abbey. Their excuse is, if you can believe it, because it makes them imagine things.

Instead of the '*as the crow flies*' routes home – via the straight highways left behind by the Romans, the children will pretend to have their parents' permission to persuade the coachman to turn off and use the crooked, winding, overgrown country lanes. Muddy and full of potholes as they are, they provide the thrilling experience of jolting shocks. Their fascination at seeing the occasional scurvy-infested rustic pulling along behind him a wife loaded up like a packhorse, staggering off in the direction of some country market, is hard to fathom. Somehow they seem almost to pray to see lurking bandits and maiden-eating dragons; lives not held in shape by Reason, but thrown to the world for adventure.

Even here in London Mrs Jervis has noticed that the instant the children's music lesson ends they will abandon Handel and Mozart in favour of some catchy, crude little ditty. Anything learned by ear, or from the street, or wafted up with the smell of burning food from the kitchen. (Oh, Visitor, is there any hope for the young? Maybe we should just give up.)

We should remind ourselves in the children's defence that all this is in the air. Since the writings of Rousseau, Nature has become a 'good guy', whereas the scheming of Man to keep his fellow man under control ('for their own good'), has been turned into a newly suspect enemy. In the last quarter of the eighteenth century, especially with the shock of the French Revolution, *Down to Earth* is the fashionable direction; girls are sometimes dressed in cotton muslin instead of silk.

The children are kept high and sheltered from the Real World in order to preserve the innocence thought necessary to keep them 'gentle'. Their parents have recently noticed how they often look down to see it *all* – but with cows, goats and all its strife – with a softer and more liberal eye than the previous generation. From up here, with mankind now arranged before Nature as a backdrop, with our heart performing its role within our intelligence, we can emerge with the children into the Romantic age – we can imagine the 'Picturesque'.

Proof of the Pudding

I once heard Edward Jervis scold his son's tutor: *'The Mind is not a vessel to be filled; but a fire to be kindled!'* I was later told that the word *education* means just that: to inspire the mind to reach out and then take in.

Whereas Edward Jervis's role in fatherhood is to remind his children of their strengths and thus to instil strategy, Mrs Jervis's role is to modify this by advising them as to their weaknesses. Just imagine one without the other! He was clever in employing architecture as a kind of big-screen demonstration of man's abilities. For instance, he explained how Reason will advise them that it is irrational to build anything which points up because it is so exposed to the elements that it will eventually be worn away and forced to fall. In Classical architecture, each course up – from the ground to the roof – is graduated *out* in order to protect the course below it. Intelligent.

The children's first pilgrimage upon their arrival in Bath each season was to walk up on to the mound of earth at the centre of the Circus and to shout their own names. They then awaited the thrill of hearing them returned to them in the round, from all directions, by way of an echoing acoustic. The Circus, their father would then explain, is a perfect circle of fine houses built to human scale – so enlarged to be *just the right* size, scale and proportions. So *right*, that the space joins in to create a WHOLE. Hearing their own voices in so tight an acoustic was, for Edward and his children, the scientific proof of the Golden Rule realised: that Man has the taste and ability to regulate harmony in the space between.

However, the problem that Edward Jervis came across in introducing the arts is the same one that we have met; it's so flat that the children's passions are beginning to play up. God is love: love is warmth; God is UP; the architecture of the Old Faith was firmly fixed in the Protestant mind as spiky *Gothic* – with phenomena like Bath Abbey left behind as relics. The enlightened architecture of an enlightened Protestant faith is intelligent Classicism. And even though everyone is busy writing and singing hymns to fire them up into a spiritual mood, how can one achieve this with a church built like a pagan temple? How can you make it look like a *Christian* church to the man in a London street? The answer is to start stacking temples.

And that is precisely what the London churches of the Wren Period of the seventeenth to the early eighteenth century did, with their famous steeples and spires.

Each afternoon the family's horses were given their exercise, and if neither of their parents needed the coach, the children were sent off with their governess to 'take the air'. As they charged about the capital, with Miss Sophie J. dashing back and forth between windows treading on everyone's toes to the melody of an imagined violin descant, the other children were made to look out and study. Rebecca did her bit by sending them off at the front door with: '*Remember! The angry look down; the dull – straight ahead; and the inspired – up.*'

They saw at once how the poorer London parishes had brought their churches up to date simply by adding to the top of their square medieval tower a little wooden structure, like the one atop St Mary's Rotherhithe, in the shape of a temple. These are often painted with lead white to preserve the wood from the elements. Now what was once square can begin to point. Easy. But then, starting anew, the children saw the simplest Tuscan temple imaginable with no steeple at all: St Paul's, *Covent Garden*. From there, all the fun was on the rise.

St Paul's

Christchurch, Spitalfields

St Brides

St Leonard's Shoreditch

St Paul's Covent Garden

St George's, Bloomsbury

Up, up and away, to St Bride's, *Fleet Street*, where Sir Christopher Wren reaches for the stars. So obvious and yet so honest, this perfectly tiered spire inspired a local baker to rise to the occasion and stack cakes for weddings, also in graduating sizes of diminution, to

195

create his popular 'Brides Cakes'. And like the chimneypiece in their home Drawing Room, this cake marked the union between two sides.

Then on to their own parish church: Nicholas Hawksmoor's mighty Christ Church, *Spitalfields*. *To boldly go* – the tower starts off as a magnificent Roman triumphal arch, then graduates up; again and again, and again – until finally the whole Classical adventure gives up and, in effect, comes clean, to admit to being a soaring Gothic spire.

(*Wheee!*) – And trotting past St George's, *Bloomsbury*, they just manage to catch sight of the eighth-century BC Temple of Mausolus at Halicarnassus. And placed high atop the steps of its pyramid, all togged out in a toga and sandals, our very own Protestant import, make no mistake – from Hanover, George I. The tower is positioned back and over to one side, like an Italian campanile, so that the church's advertisement in intelligent Classical temple-fronted symmetry is not interrupted by anything vertical! And all in *Bloomsbury*? (*Phew!*)

Now to George Dance the Elder's St Leonard's, *Shoreditch*. Also ambitious, but with so many English classicists hiding in corners for fear of hearing the word 'sissy' shouted their way, this architect surprised everyone by using actual references and yet, at the same time, dared to make it all look pretty. On top of a pedestal goes a galleried colonnade, and on top of that the Temple of the Winds. Now up to a hexagonal pedestal, topped by a gallery on which rest four balls, and then on top of that an obelisk, crowned by a practical, scientific, Protestant wind vane instead of a cross. (*Whooppee!*)

The ultimate and perhaps the most interesting, and certainly the one which kept the children studying it for the rest of their lives, was St Paul's Cathedral itself. From the ground it forms into a square 'hierarchical' foundation, to serve Man's practical needs, but one which is also fashioned upon the lines of the Latin cross. Then what was once square rises up and up until it is rounded off in its preparation for the great summit of Heaven's Gate, with the very ideal of God's spherical grace symbolised in the form of a dome. On top, in gold, is a *vertical* line crossed *horizontally* by another, but fixed at a point slightly *higher*, rather than *lower*. Not just a Latin cross, it is the orb of God's Dominion. Just imagine, the story of the children's own lives, from birth to death, but told from bottom to top by one structure in Portland stone.

Its great clock ticks and tocks, but it also strikes the quarter hour – just like the little one at home. The children insist that St Paul has a great big ding-dong. Silly things.

CHAPTER SIXTEEN

STATE VISIT: MIND TO HEART

When we look up at the house from the street, if the *piano nobile* is the belly of a town house, then surely the next floor up, the second, must contain its heart. A journey to the heart of any house is to the private place that holds its owner by night: the master's bedchamber is the house's emotional core. Up here, by the cosiness of their chamber's fire, the Jervises sometimes remind their children that 'hearth' is an ancient English word meaning *heart*. ¶ By the same reasoning, and also by being up so high, we might feel ourselves safely separated from the real world below. After all, the front hall, various floors and several reception rooms are all standing between us and the front door, all of which, so you might remember, have developed historically in the retreating quest for more privacy, warmth, safety and light. The *chamber* before us is the safe place descended from a castle *keep*; now the house's heart, in it are stored the master and his most prized and personal possessions – including (sometimes) a wife. If the hall was the opening to our visit, and the Drawing Room a social halfway house, then what lies ahead of us now must be the ultimate destination.

As we stand before the door, I suggest that you might imagine taking me into the region around your own bed at home. Unlike the other rooms with their social nature, this space is an intimate and private domain which we sense we should enter only by invitation. Here society ends and intimacy begins: something I believe you are about to feel.

What your intelligence has so far experienced in this house is an age-old power trip called a *parade*. Its objective is basically manipulative: to control for the sake of safety and order. It works at its purest, or most obvious, in the layout of a good bordello where a client is led past a display of expensive watches, jewellery, clothing – as well as an impressive array of glamorous photographs – all painting an impressive image, all very definitely laid out to impress someone . . . on their way to bed.

Great stately homes, like Blenheim Palace, Chatsworth House, Hampton Court Palace and Windsor Castle, are *parade houses* in that a visit to them is designed to be a psychological experience. Each room is conceived to work on a visitor's sensibilities in a way that capitalises on the psychology perfected into high art by Louis XIV at Versailles. From the layout of ancient cave decorations we can see that even in prehistoric times the same format of unfolding drama was employed to control those who entered from outside.

Though I draw no direct parallel, I can see enough of your features in the faint light to know that something about the way I describe the parade sounds a little familiar.

First there comes a grand but rather awesome arrival: in London those horse-drawn carriage processions through streets decorated with flags and lined with saluting guardsmen, shouting captains, firing of guns and pealing of bells. Made nervous by so much *brutta grandezza*, the visitor is then taken on foot up a great stair to a floor above the world. A pair of magnificent doors open and the visitor – now a parader – begins to make his way in, deeper and deeper, away from the real world into one of private splendour. first you might pass flexing displays of the owner's power and might: armour, weaponry and military trophies. Intimidated, you will now behave better, and appear more refined. Slowly you progress through a succession of rooms, each ceremonially paraded through, each becoming grander and more impressive.

Such refinement! Such symmetry! You are awed by the owner's personal taste and read it as an advertisement of his or her integrity; hopefully it will all lead to the establishment of trust. The plot thickens as organised collections fill each room: one packed with Chinese porcelain; a gallery hung with fine pictures; a 'blue room'; a 'gold room' – your procession now moves down a corridor that plays on light, reflections and shadows – called a *hall of mirrors*. And finally you stand before the door to your final destination: the room where the owner of such magnificence actually dwells in person. In you go – and there it is: the bed itself; the spectacular place where he or she is so safe that they dare leave and then re-enter consciousness. Now you, the exhausted, awestruck and bewildered parader, stand overwhelmed; you are putty in your host's hands – whose excuse is, just as is mine, that all this is good for you. Sound familiar?

201

Just a minute . . . 'Knock knock!'

Before such a door in this house I now stand, with my little ball of putty standing beside me – we are all ready to roll.

'*Inside that room*', I say with an awed nod, '*our master and mistress are contained. The bed itself is probably the house's most important possession. So high – and at the front facing the street, with servants kept below until summoned, the Master's sword and all his keys so near . . . it reminds one of state rituals.*'

By now we both recognise Sophie's chamber-stick as an official invitation. A little cautiously I stoop down to peek through the keyhole. No, still there. Not yet. I knock and after a suitable pause I reach forward and crack open the door. More darkness, more caution, in there even the walls have ears. I lift the chamber-stick to use its light and as I do a warmth containing the smell of wax and smoke comes at us, as if the room's lights have only just been extinguished. Our couple have hurried off to hide. Or, at least, so our speeding hearts make us imagine.

We enter.

State Arrival

The light flashes to expose disjointed glimpses of an extraordinary room. Curtains cascade from the ceiling down over the windows, like the satin that falls out of Heaven in allegories. Soft celestial colours – the Mediterranean pinks and blues cringed at by earlier Protestants – are on view for the first time; gold adorns every surface, to catch the light as it moves. A huge, heavy-baroque mantelpiece, bending beneath the weight of a mountain of exotic blue and white china, stands tall at the far end of the room – but not quite, we notice, at the centre. And on our right a shrine-like lady's dressing table that almost bids us kneel before it with a rosary. And yes, there it is,

the grandest upholstered baroque four-poster bed imaginable. Hung with yellow and red damask curtains trimmed in red braid, with corners fashioned to protect in scrolls and coils punctuated with hanging cords and tassels of every size – all faded, but we can still see that they were once so fanciful as to be brilliant. Somewhere, surely, the ghosts of ancient cavemen chiefs, Roman emperors, a host of good 'escorts' and Louis XIV, must be standing in the shadow to see its effect; we have arrived and stand wide-eyed. No longer are they *our* Mr and Mrs Jervis: now – we are *theirs*.

And just what's happened to the refinement of taste then? Or so a certain expression would seem to ask. Looking around you: too old, too much, certainly not 'just right'. But then again nothing is actually *wrong* with it all either. What is it?

Footsteps! Someone is coming up the stairs! *'Quickly,'* I say, grabbing you by one arm and gesturing to the front right-hand corner of the room, where there stands a large screen covered in pearl-white damask. Without you seeing me, I rather nimbly reach for a fishing wire concealed behind one of the bedposts and begin to tug. As the door magically begins to draw open (wink, wink) I push you in its direction to feel you tense up, before making you duck backward to shelter behind the screen. The very idea of being caught in someone's bedroom . . .!

Kicking a pair of my own socks out of sight, I whisper, *'She has returned. Now listen carefully,'* adding, *'to her voice and all.'*

'I thought that you might feel you know us more intimately by seeing more of the house. Even if – in private – we are so disappointingly old-fashioned.' It is the voice of Elizabeth Jervis with a gentleman and a lady, who as a part of their visit seemed to have earned the privilege of seeing beyond the Drawing Room. Their voices suggest that they are both delighted and charmed by the household and what they see.

'Awe! . . . must have heard us coming.
Come on! . . . they've gone.'

'*My toilet mirror and table were, for more than sixty years, in the possession of my dear grandmother, and still contain a good deal of her integrity. The collection of porcelain belonged to my aunt – Lady Bolingbroke – and was specially bequeathed to me, for which I am exceedingly grateful. It gives the family so much pleasure. Because of it my husband has been inspired to develop a taste for porcelain, and I am told that he has a good eye and can feel its age. We never tire of gazing at it in the delight of noticing something new. The children have added their own contributions,*' – this we hear while sensing her smile. '*Over half of it fell one night and had to be glued together.*' We hear the rustle of a sleeve as she points to the small squidgy mound of cow gum to our right, with broken fragments of china projecting from it, and adds, '*This one was mended by our youngest daughter, Miss Sophie Jervis.*

'*The carpet is a good one in that it does not show the dirt. Once a fortnight we sweep it with damp tealeaves to restore the pile. I believe it is Egyptian, or perhaps Mexican, or somewhere from that region. I cannot for the life of me remember.*' I dig my elbows into your side. '*It is turned upside down during the whole of the month of March to encourage the sand to fall out in the same direction as it entered. And our cook is very good at painting out the worn spots with ink.*' We hear the knowing humour in her voice.

'*It is a strange tale that our bed hangings were a commission placed by my grandfather with my husband's father, for the visit of a royal guest to the family house in Spital Yard in 1707; later they were presented to us both by my grandmother on our wedding night. Given the choice, we would never have allowed ourselves such an extravagance.*' She laughs. '*The honest, but very simple, chairs are from my husband's family and still give us good service. The sturdy old tea table was used by his mother, and he takes much comfort in having so important a family piece as he can remember from his youth still so close by. With the world and the silk trade in such turmoil, the chamber is our escape: we love it here – so.*'

So we hear a gracious, mild, honest-voiced Elizabeth Jervis speak with love of her own chamber. We stoop side by side to look down into the dark to listen and imagine the party leaving this room for the one next door: Mrs Jervis's boudoir.

. . . walls . . . have ears.

The Jervises – By Heart

Upon slipping back into the room you peer around you with a new style of more inspired interest. I take Sophie's light and travel from candle to candle, bringing the room to life. You ask me why tea has been slopped into all of the saucers. Bending forward to inspect more closely I explain that Mrs Jervis does this automatically just before she leaves a room to ensure that – this time – Rebecca will wash the saucers *as well* as the cups. Charmed, you smile. Yes, now it all seems very different: more human, more individual, more personal.

Their bed: the place where our couple leave and re-enter consciousness – its linen sheets still tossed back – you can somehow still *feel* their near-presence. Spread over a billowing white damask tablecloth is the silver and porcelain they used for their breakfast, by the look of it only a short while ago. Crumbs, napkins, toasted bread with bites missing, a boiled egg with a spoon still projecting from it, coffee – we smell before we see. It is only half taken.

Onward go your eyes: to the fire, which still smoulders; to Elizabeth's face screen hanging on its left, and to Edward's boots propped up to dry, on the right. Even the chamber pot sits ready to be emptied, while a sprig of lavender, half burnt, lies ready to freshen the air. Far off in the distance someone on horseback – now so late – rides up and then on by.

I replenish the fire. *'Everything is so . . . vertical. Colours that lift the heart, taken from the sea and sky. Passions for things: flowers and exotic oriental porcelain, children's toys and what must have been a kind of family "levée". Downstairs was so formal, so flat. Here, so sheltered,'* – so I say, almost with a laugh, *'I guess . . . we are intended to* feel *high or low.'*

Out of the Blue

The colour white is meant to represent right now: no mystery for things before, nothing after, only now. This room is the very opposite. In the air here is the colour of romance: a hue somewhere between blue and white. Whether in blue jeans or porcelain, the reason that blue and white are so universally popular as a pair of colours is that the combination transports the imagination 'over' – whether by sea or by sky – to Somewhere Else.

We move our chairs up closer to the fire and to each other, so that we can speak in a more personal, softer tone. Every once in a while there is heard a domestic sound: a clock being wound, a voice on the stairs, someone fumbling at the door. *'That child again: the midget.'* I rise and sneak over to lock the latch.

You sit and gaze above you at the huge and heavy baroque mantelpiece, as visitors tend to do, and above it to the tiered stacks of old blue and white china which bank right up to the ceiling. I add another log to the fire and gently adjust my voice to intercept your thoughts and – just for a moment – lead your imagination off on our first *romantic* excursion: one that insists that you temporarily – but completely – abandon Reason. 'China Blue' is an imaginary oriental city that sits high upon the rocks, crags and cliffs overlooking the China Sea.

'Listen,' I begin. *'Hear the gulls, the lapping water and the popping creaks of our wooden junk? Feel the balmy breeze scooping at our sails as we are blown so gently in. Alas – the Orient! Look! Just as the Jervises always imagined it – too. An entire city built of the finest porcelain: with turrets and towers, gates and walls: its citizens have come out to stand, watch and wave us in. Everyone is porcelain. Tiered right up – stacked from the harbour on the rocks, right up into the mountains – to disappear into clouds, to somewhere near the seat of Gods.'*

Someone once waved. But if I had tried that out on you any earlier? Well, it seems to have worked on you well enough now; and your imagination is that much rounder because of it. This is the *emotional taste* that we need as fuel for the rest of our journey. And in being so, we are not alone. *Romance* too found its Time.

Sudden interest?
Our couple were wed at Christ Church, Spitalfields, on 2 June 1761. He a Whig, she a Tory; he – Protestant dissenter, she an Anglican! To imagine the union will take two hands.

CHAPTER SEVENTEEN

LOVE AT THE CENTRE

Both the Jervises, cultivated by Reason and with no rough edges, share a natural gift for balance. From their marriage on, in terms of their Passions, it is enough to know that Edward Jervis is the fiction of your right hand, and can be imagined to employ all those twitches and initiatives that give things life. Whereas Elizabeth St John Jervis is the steadying and modifying left hand, essential to keeping things on the right track. Radiating from the centre is the bonding warmth they call love. Both are easy to love. ¶ Oh, and theirs was a love match – all right. Edward and Elizabeth Jervis shared this same great bed throughout their marriage, the first generation on either side of the family – within living memory – to do so. Previously, as we might have suspected, a successful marriage was one which proved to be a good working relationship – with the added bonus that the pair ended up fond of and loyal to one another – as in the contract made with the wedding vow. And in the case of 'arranged marriages', with property or politics being the first consideration, all the usual causes of eventual emotional stress were thought omitted to begin with. Oh, so they said.

As we seat ourselves in their two chairs, I poke at the fire to reveal that the couple do, however, have their *ups and downs*.* I explain that Edward feels that God is in his soul. From there he feels warmth, and he is closest to it when engaged in good practical work: hence his noted work ethic. His focus is more down-to-earth and practical. His religion is that of the low dissenter and politically he favours the Whigs.

If Edward Jervis built England, it would have to resemble Holland or Germany from the air: organised by practical straight roads and rectangular fields. If he splintered off to begin a new life in America – as so many of his persuasion did – his Puritan energy would have him lay the streets of his new land out in a practical grid pattern, with its civic buildings standing like temples at its intersections.

If Elizabeth Jervis were responsible for building England, it would look from the air like a patchwork of oddly shaped fields and meandering lanes – as if Nature herself had advised her on the gentlest and least confrontational forms of layouts and routes. On

---

* The domestic scenes described in this chapter, and the next, can move in your imagination to Bach's Brandenburg Concertos. It was within them, listened to continuously during the house's restoration, that these instances were first observed.

the other hand, Elizabeth's is not a religion, but a 'faith'. Her God is felt to be high and constant, and is not conditional on any effort: she is a High Anglican and a Tory.

Her parish church is Christ Church, which points up to the sky. The word prayer means *connection*, and when she prays she points her fingers upward, like folk in medieval paintings, whereas Edward's hands are tightly clasped, neat and square; like his chapel at the opposite end of the same street, and like nonconformist chapels in general.

While adding another log to the fire I explain, *'If either of the two structures had voices, then Church and Chapel would resemble our couple. Her voice is high, like that of a cathedral choir, and his is deep and solid, like a Welsh choir of Methodist miners. This energy dictates the overall shape of his body and the pull of his features: a practical height and weight, balanced from the centre, like a rugby player. Her features and shape are drawn upward, tall and slim.'*

. . . and, they're off!

I advise you to take hold of your own two hands as – in two-two time – off they go! Suddenly we hear voices and footsteps as the domestic sounds return from every direction to make the whole house spin to life around us. With our couple kept neatly concealed behind the screen my voice also slips into two-two time:

'*Left! – Right! – Left!* . . . Mrs Jervis *manages to lie in;* Mr Jervis *can't help* but rise with the dawn. He looks *competent,* she *at ease.* He speeds up when you stare at him; she slows down. He *makes* things happen, she *allows* them to be. He *raises* Rebecca's wages, she grants a '*rise*'. He will warn you in advance, she when it's too late. He *mounts the attack,* she *stands her ground.* He *makes mistakes,* she . . . *forgets.* Trouble, and he is *forced to swear* while she *holds her tongue.* He breathes *out –* she breathes *in.* He will *call the whole thing off;* she will contrive a scheme of *terminal postponement.* He is accused of *justifiable arrogance,* she of *false modesty.* I shake my head to conclude, '*Such a handful!*'

Love, at Home

In the pleasant peace that follows your eye begins to wander. For, by knowing where the couple are coming from, or so to speak, you begin to see something more. That the house is a coalition of two *emotional* tastes. The formal symmetry of the ceiling in the Drawing Room is, of course, *his,* whereas the meandering rococo one on the first Landing must be *hers. His* furniture is new, made of mahogany as an investment: somehow it improves with age. *Hers* is higher, older and bolder, some of it quirky, exuberant and even theatrical. It is distanced from her by inheritance. In a class of its own.

Yes . . . which mirror; which pattern on which piece of upholstery; which colour painted on which wall? Now, suddenly, I suspect that you may see it all. In fact, by knowing Mr and Mrs Jervis your eye might well wander off all over England. For, *by design* – from topiary to 'crazy paving' – maybe the WHOLE PICTURE OF ENGLAND is supposed to start from here?

Behold, a mystery

'Why the screen?' you ask. Your attention is drawn to the corner of the room and the screen we hid behind earlier. I take hold of your sleeve and tug you back down into your seat to ask, *'If we peek, what if, instead of Mrs Jervis, we find an actress holding a script? Too tall, too short . . . a different race or colour? An American! . . . the Duchess of York? . . . then what?'*

I explain that what we know of them we have met halfway. So far they have been made of the very best, and not the very worst of us. God, the Jervises, big stars and royalty – they know exactly what they are doing when they keep their distance. *'If you think about it, it all happens in the space between; to which both sides project their best – or their worst – for the effect of a central prize. If we actually see them, reason alone will take control and any mystery will dissolve. Our story, any story, will be over.'*

I release your sleeve. We both turn away and face the hearth. I say, *'The night is turning cold, but our fire is burning well.'* Holding my two hands up to it I encourage you to do the same. You do. *'Nice and warm.'*

Watching your eye taken by Mrs Jervis's dress, I float some words into the space and check your response; seeing I am welcome to speak, and that I am not trespassing on your own picture. *'They both dress outwards in layers; she with petticoats (quilted in winter), and finally with an "open robe" on top, like that one, there. Some say they've seen her in the magnificent "Robe Polonaise", which is on display in the Victoria and Albert Museum, and which inspired the decorator John Fowler to revive the legendary "festoon" – or "knickers curtains" – that so suffocated the 1980s.'*

You look across to the dressing table as if to ask for more. Why the pennies half-hidden under the cloth?

'Pin money . . . hidden from a certain servant's temptations?' I explain that

in the same way as modern dress designers still do, Mrs Jervis pins together 'a look' whenever she dresses; in the same way that she created her Drawing Room curtains. This is what others of her own sex often look out for as her '*touch*'. The rest of what she wears can be bought.

You sniff. '*Her scent.*' But you look down your nose, at the smell of eau de Cologne, I explain that spirit was the only cheap and cheerful gift that the allied troops, stationed in Cologne at the end of the Seven Years War, could find or afford to bring home to their womenfolk. The whole of London and of Europe stinks of it. At the same time I run my finger across a ledge in search of dust. '*Nicely kept*; very *clean. Now, isn't it a pleasant smell?*' You have to think. And after a short pause I ask, '*But what if the room were filthy? Would you trust that smell? Or would you suspect it as covering over something unpleasant? Maybe even vile?*'

I gesture towards a certain couple concealed behind the screen. '*Are we dirty until we are cleansed? – as "take the bull by the horns" Mr Edward Jervis would tell you we are? Or are we clean before something unnatural – like a government or a church – steps in to make us dirty? As the "wait-and-see" Mrs Jervis would tell us it is.*' We ponder High or Low; for which is right?

Looking down at my own hands I say, '*I don't know about you, but I find the style of their animation, their "manner", differs so in the way I picture each of them.*' As a log rolls over, I concentrate more intensely on the flames. '*In Edward's case it's, well, not "etiquette", but the opposite: he is gracious, almost quaint, old-fashioned, "genteel". Is there a name? Oh, I know, "Chivalry".*'

'Court' manners filter down to where they eventually become anchored in pretension. The manners of chivalry, on the other hand, are not pretentious. They are the manners of male conduct softened by the hearts of the knights of old; they too are frozen to remain classic.

We are both silent with our own thoughts, before I add that chivalry must have been the classless manners taken by the Puritans to the American Colonies. I remember my father opening doors and holding himself back for others when they wished to pass; the way men would always seat their wives, sometimes even placing their coats over their shoulders. And of course, chivalry's greatest legacy – the meal they all made of a good handshake. All so quaintly performed, almost as if somehow, somewhere (and I narrow my eyes to search back), there might have been some kind of prize, or reward, waiting in store.

You rise, walk over, and bend down to read an article related to Mrs Jervis's faith. *'As a good Christian she was brought up with her generation on the analogy of "JOY"*: Jesus – *first*; Others – *second*; and Yourself – *last.'* I ask, *'Is that not – even with her high manner – what is at the root of her aristocratic charm? A kind of distanced humility, by deflection?'*

The World Turned Upside Down

As the fire pops and crackles, I rise to step on a spark and then walk over to lean with both hands on the back of a chair to see the dressing table for myself. I say, *'The Countess of Coventry is dying of cosmetic poisoning. Her insecurity has led her to cover herself under mountains of lead and mercury-based make-up. As she grows more ill, the more she uses to conceal it. The moral of the tragedy is much taken up by a "Macaroni" society, somehow sensing that they may be drifting too far off the mark: haunted by the call of the alternative direction, back to Nature.'* Adding *'. . . now so suddenly seen as good!'*

Hearing the sound of a proud horse trotting through the street

– I float, *'General Washington went to London, riding on a pony. Stuck a feather in his hat and called it Macaroni.'* What hope is there now, in 1780, for peace between high England and its closer to the earth American Colonies? By now the two sides are even dressing as enemies. The Colonists dress like an old-fashioned people left behind in a time warp from the Puritan Commonwealth, the British like old-style Cavaliers, at their most outrageous, with the macaronis in their red coats, paint and powder.

Walking to the window, I peek out from around the edge of the blind to say of passers-by, *'By and large only the well-to-do and "cads" still wear wigs; and to pay for the American war a tax on hair powder has made the wig and the powdering finally begin to disappear.'* Looking at my own hand, *'Man versus Nature – and Nature is winning.'* Adding, *'Eventually it always will.'*

Down!

I close my eyes to see Edward Jervis wearing his own hair, by now a little grey. Before, he joined the two front sides of his shirt with a simple cravat instead of a long scarf knotted into a xounce; but soon this will develop into a necktie, which is safer for riding, work and sport. Dressed without pocket watch, for those too are taxed to pay for the American war. I whisper that he should be careful not to go out without his tax receipt, for London is crawling with informers who live by the rewards. Those clocks we see in London are only just now being affixed to its church towers in order to 'give England back its time'.

'*And Mrs Jervis?*' With this I hold up my gentler left hand to smile and say, '*"Big hair", a tasteful version of the "macaroni", right the way through the war; coping – but never complaining: using flour instead of powder – never gave an inch.*'

The Thunder Begins to Roll

Funny . . . Old Isaac used to claim that when a number of earthquakes rocked London in the 1750s, the Wesleyan chapels were suddenly packed to capacity. Well, in 1794, it has taken the Revolution in France to make everyone stand back to see just how High and Low things have drifted. The family are reading daily reports of the Reign of Terror: the most illustrious Court in Christendom carted through the streets of Paris and publicly executed! What was once regarded as 'colourful' has suddenly turned on itself, to be sickened by its own excess, and fashion is now galloping down in the direction of the wholesome and virtuous. I draw closer. Last July – in the year of Marie Antoinette's execution –

everyone at once made the quick switch from silk to simple printed cottons and muslins; the silk-weavers here were thrown into a state of near starvation. I lower my voice to mumble, 'Rioting is again erupting, the king's troops and the local militias are sent in almost daily; downstairs the shutters are barred at nightfall.' Suddenly the smell of scent has become uncomfortable, the smell of plain soap better: but no smell at all is just right.

We both close our eyes to see more. With all the bad news, are the daughters not 'tossing' their hair instead of confecting the perfect mountain they used to toil over, with pelmets of flags, forts and ships and birdcages? So shaken by the drama, are they not wearing necklaces of thin red riband high up around their necks to represent the guillotine? That is, before, so taste asks me to add, *'their father caught sight of it and made them throw them on the fire? The word "citizen" is being used as a term of abuse for a certain style of upstart who has little talent for wealth and power, a word banned here on grounds of unstructured taste.'*

The colour red on the first landing has now been painted out. To the sensitive, gilding suddenly feels outrageous, as it did to many eyes after both world wars. The pedestal, column and capital seemed too instructively formal in young William Jervis's eye, and it was he who began a campaign to cover over the Drawing Room panelling – first with calico, and then over that with wallpaper, decorated of course, with natural motifs and patterns of meandering flowers. Thus there came a liberating victory by the heart over the order and strategy of the mind, here and in panelled rooms all over town: a revolution.

I tell you how I once heard his father, Edward Jervis, maintain that man was separated from the beasts by Reason, but that I have recently heard him state a rounder truth. *'What need have the beasts of Reason – if indeed they are empowered with instincts? Man is separated from the beasts, make no mistake – by* sentiment.' Apparently, it was something warm, *between* the bones, which came forth to tell him so.

All this I tell you because I feel you meeting it, and me, halfway. If I feel you withdraw I will know to stop. This sensitivity is provided by the heart, the emotional taste that is – by the late eighteenth century – a new skill.

As the cat somehow manages to push open the door I explain how people are now posing far more often in natural or half-outdoors settings, often with animals somewhere nearby. The cat joins in to make our little fireside scene 'picturesque'. I add that despite the goodness of Nature the painter Thomas Gainsborough still prefers to work inside his studio rather than out of doors: he uses broccoli as the model for his famous trees.

Again I rise and peek out from behind the blind to the street, where we can hear the watchmen crying out a late, late hour. In a low voice: *'Up in town, since the Gordon Riots of 1780, against concessions to the Catholics, there is considerable suspicion. The king had the windows of his coach smashed yesterday as he rode to Parliament through a crowd chanting, "Bread! Bread! Bread!" He must now revel in his humbled reputation as "Farmer George": it might save his and his family's necks. Down in the country, it looks as if the crops are again going to fail: flour will soon have to be rationed for anything except bread. The potter Wedgwood will soon manufacture pottery pastry shells in which the posh can serve their pie meats.'* Guardedly I mumble, *'In nearby Loom Court a woman has been found dead bending beside a tin containing a potato, placed over what would have been a fire of only two sticks, had it not refused to light.'*

I come closer and lower my voice to describe the shouts of the mob, in red caps, who chant outside Christ Church each Sunday and who are becoming louder and louder each week. So also are the troops who deal with them getting tougher and tougher. On a

Sunday morning in 1794 our family had bull's blood cast over their clothes and their coach was pelted with bottles as they left after divine service. *'Pushed and pulled. Up or down. So difficult to keep repose: to keep to the centre.'*

In – to the Centre

Recently a list of the Seven Deadly Sins has appeared on Mrs Jervis's dressing table. The gift of her husband, apparently it is these seven things – pride, lust, anger, gluttony, sloth, envy, covetousness – that ruin a noble human repose. I ask you to experiment and to apply one of the sins to what you see of Mrs Jervis, and then watch how quickly her perfect composure is lost. Wide-eyed we gaze into the fire. It's true.

I disclose that I once heard her warning her eldest daughter never to allow the eye the freedom to look too closely at the things that mar the faces of others. *'An eye thus trained only to the surface – and no deeper, is sure one day to turn upon* itself.'

Ding – dong! As the clock on the landing strikes the quarter hour I lift the poker and point to the waxed finish on a chair leg that has caught the golden glow of the fire. Rich – honey-brown, like the one we once knew in the air of the kitchen, but here with a hint of red and orange – like the seed of a horse chestnut newly opened from its shell. Funny isn't it? As time goes on the Jervises, like their mahogany, seem to have stopped shining and begun to glow. I once heard it explained that some woods contain an acid which makes them go dry, dull and mark. Those that have no acid, nothing inside to sour and turn on them, grow more beautiful with age.

The silence makes us aware of someone in the distance practising upon a new *piano-forte*. Unlike the *harpsichord*, this newer

instrument has been more recently invented to project and regulate passion by way of percussion, and we can hear it being played very well to that effect. What began by soothing the symmetry of our mind, has now, like poetry in words, curved round to pleasing our hearts as well. Hypnotic, both sensations provided by the same piece by Haydn, have succeeded in catching in such a way to make us – dream.

Nevertheless we sit side by side to gaze at the closed blinds and contemplate the dawn of a new day in Romantic time. Beyond, a blackbird sings to the peal of bells that flies in the same breeze; somehow people fit into what we see outside too. I notice that we hold our right hands in our left, as a contented warmth makes us both begin to smile. Nature is good; God and Love are here aligned. There is Harmony *between*.

CHAPTER EIGHTEEN

THE LIGHTS GO OUT

We hear Edward Jervis's voice behind the screen; he is in prayer. *Up and Down, Back and Forth* – now *In and Out*. Our creation is apparently by now so three-dimensional that he should be able to stand and walk on his own. As with any work of art, grown-up adult or new nation, he too will no longer need us, or anyone else, to tell him what is right or wrong. He is *connected* and can therefore set forth into Time alone. It is best now to slip away and leave him in the Time we invented him to suit. ¶ On Sunday 26 November 1811 prayers were given and the news announced from the pulpits of both church and chapel that silk master Edward Jervis was gravely ill. Straw had

to be scattered in Folgate Street to deaden the sound of footsteps
and horses so that he might better rest. Later on the same day the
beadle and watchman for the Liberty closed it and other adjoining
streets when word was received that any *horizontal* hope of his
recovery had now been abandoned in favour of *vertical* resolve.
Edward Jervis adhered to his fate impressively, and with his

permission several hundred weavers packed the street outside the house at dusk to sing some of his favourite old weavers' songs, including the great Huguenot anthem – sung in rounds – which moved him so. His inner spirit – by this – thus lifted, he was ready.

We emerge from behind the screen into a darkened chamber with a cold hearth and take the positions advised to us by our instincts: to face each other from either side of the same great bed and make it the stage for a hero's demise.

Together we stand to close our eyes and listen to the eerie mystery of the muffled drums and the gruesome peal of clapped bells spinning out over the roofs and chimneys of Spitalfields. By the light of a full moon we catch sight of a stately vision: we see a stately night procession, with solemn and heavily cloaked paid mourners preceding Edward – like mobile statues with bowed heads – who navigate inward towards the eye. Before and aft, and in formal half-step, we watch the lighted flares and gold-tipped staffs offered up around a funeral car upholstered in powder-black and gold, moving past rows of bare and bowed heads; past the same number again – packed indoors – of women, children and servants, who stand to watch from behind uneven window panes in respectfully darkened rooms of those old houses along his route.

In the Boudoir
(From 1811-ish, to 1830-ish)

We depart for the future with his widow, by moving through to the sunny little room on the south side of this floor: what used to be her boudoir, or dressing room. It is this place which contains our next spell. We listen for her to depart, and after having heard her and her close friend and neighbour Mrs James Stilwell stop their chat and

233

down their teacups, we open a tiny communicating door concealed in one corner of the chamber.

A canary begins to sing as the room brings a new, almost liberating sensation. Fresh colours of apricot, cream-white and sky blue. A smell of toasted scones, blended with a touch of scent. Powerfully feminine, and so personal, from *here* the past we have left behind suddenly seems Spartan. It may only be the insecurity caused by Mr Jervis's death, but how good all this looks and feels; and how quickly I see you melt to its charm! A newly installed hob grate has been fitted to the fire to accommodate coal and it burns away more efficiently than ever a fire did before: the room is as warm as toast. The sabre backs on the chairs seem to encourage a more relaxed posture, and unlike the great bed that dominated the centre of the old Chamber, here a daybed sits sideways along one wall, like a divan, offering an unspoken invitation to recline. How tempting it is; to remove our outer layers, and as it is fully carpeted, perhaps our shoes

as well? Even if not, how nice it is to be invited to relax. Just in from the past, we are more than glad to meet with such comfort.

With the two ladies' footsteps and voices now halfway down the stairs, we make a move to seat ourselves in their chairs, and find that the seats are still warm. Before us, on the little oval Pembroke table, their tea is still steaming in the cups. Above us to one side, draped over the dressing-table mirror, is a piece of silk from Mrs Jervis's wedding dress – woven by her husband on his own loom, by his own hand. On the mantelshelf are the last battered remains of the 'creamware' dishes which she used to teach her children to take tea with, before allowing them to join the smart company, with smarter porcelain, in the Drawing Room. The newer pieces commemorate a peace treaty with Napoleon as well as the tragic death of Princess Charlotte of Wales in childbirth; black mourning ribbons suggest that Mrs Jervis has joined the nation in being deeply affected by this tragedy. A collection of famous signatures in frames has been hung, of course, *very* symmetrically, and on her dressing table stands a miniature portrait of Mrs Jervis herself, executed in charcoal, drawn in the year of her marriage, 1761.

Such comfort must be a reward made to us by Time, for previously such personal things, even this degree of feminine softness, were kept purposely at bay when we were downstairs, under the spell of Reason. All this would have then been thought unhealthy, even decadent. However, it feels good to sit amongst things that require a dialogue of tender acceptance between hearts.

Knee-deep in Romance

The experience of this room always reminds me of being told that when the curtains went up on any Ivor Novello musical in the 1940s the audience knew to expect the same thing. The male lead singer would leap across the stage, to fall at the feet of his leading lady, and then burst into song. Thus the mood was set, or even decreed, to be one of *romance*. So given over to Passion that Reason is pushed aside, and with women in such a position of power – just think of what might happen!

Such is our new setting: a room so lopsidedly feminine that it is almost stage-set romantic. In historic terms it might be said that women are now *getting their own back*. Femininity is no longer sheepishly edging its way in with the hope of being tolerated, but is so triumphant that newer interiors are dolled up in a way that advertises them as a woman's domain. A man's role by now is restricted to paying for everything and going down on his knees to general repairs; a role so rational as to be doomed by romance to be completely uninteresting. He will have to return to building bridges and fighting battles.

We are then, being *instructed*, as listeners are sometimes instructed by the music of the Romantic composers, to allow our hearts to triumph over Reason and step up on to a soft white cloud, to float away into a sky-blue and apricot sunset. That is, without Reason taking all the fun out of it by asking us if we have our maps, passports, money and tickets. *From here* we may join with the time to read poetry aloud, whereas in downstairs' sterner formality this might well have invited a giggle. Here, at last, Reason can no longer object to me using an exclamation mark on the cold grounds of taste.

And again somewhere in the background we hear the teasing symmetry of one of those new duets for piano-forte and cello. Right here, we can look before us at the table with its two chairs and two cups of steaming tea, and listen to the music, imagining the see-sawing niceties of the scene between Mrs Jervis and Mrs Stilwell which we have only just missed.

Here we can imagine Mrs Jervis gazing into a painting, simply because it's 'pretty' or because it persuades her mind to travel. *From here* on, if she commissions an artist to paint her grandchildren it will no longer be with the excuse of their being recorded for posterity, but because she loves them. And *from here*, think what that will do to the way she would see them pose. And especially when compared to the 'refined' look that we once stiffened up to copy. Maybe we should go to the National Gallery to see the result of this change? And can we not see our widow, sitting in that roomy, cushioned windowseat, sewing and reading in the warm morning sunlight? It may be only our imaginations, but has the windowseat actually been enlarged for such a purpose? Perhaps Jane Austen should be read there, for the true comic conflict of Reason with Passion: '*Sense and Sensibility.*'

'*In fact, from here,*' so I add with a wicked expression, '*if what we know of the Romantic Age does not comply with the spell, then history will have got it wrong. We should crawl in further, take it over, and then make damned sure that it does.*'

Taste Gets a Breath of Fresh Air

By now it would seem that the 'picturesque' is getting its own way too. For whereas older houses were built to focus inward to the hearth, and stand with their backs facing out to the world, newer houses are being built to face out of doors; some with façades that even project – or 'bow' outwards to make that point. The new focus is supposed to be the house's natural, or what is often contrived to be natural – surrounding. Regency London, as seen from the barouche of our imagination, would drive us past an almost Mediterranean backdrop of terraces and villas, all being constructed with plain brick façades, but then embellished with stucco before being painted to resemble real stone (which would be far too expensive). Mrs Jervis sees Regent's Park as pure theatre – with accommodation.

1720

1820

'Honestly!
Anyone would think . . .
by looking at houses without
piano nobile . . . *with*
"French" windows and
trellis-like wrought-iron
balconies, that men might
now be wearing trousers
instead of breeches and
hose; that women are in
pumps and dressed in
"empire" waists with
parasols!'

I am afraid that we will have to inform Reason that the sash windows it invented are far too restricting, and that bricks are being knocked out and balconies added so that windows are fast becoming 'French', to open out as doors. Some windows open out on to little wrought-iron balconies or porches, adorned with charming tent-shaped canopied roofs, like parasols, designed to protect the head portion of the body from the sun when one sits 'out'. Glazing bars are getting thinner and thinner: soon they will disappear altogether to become plate glass. And, over us, no longer the great, heavy, suffocating portcullis-type curtains, but prettily decorated and stylishly arranged un-lined cotton muslin.

So the barriers are fast being removed. Such is the invitation to our imagination to step outdoors and into an ever-enlarging picture: one that includes Nature. Indeed, instead of life as a column set up on a pedestal, newer houses are sometimes built without *piano nobile*, their reception rooms raised only slightly above the ground, near to the door and garden.

Setting You Up to Bring You Down

My word! – but aren't you comfortable! Very comfortable indeed. You seem to want to put your feet up. As you remove your jacket your eye travels across to Mrs Jervis, to notice that her clothes are far less restrictive too; a flimsier look, closer to Nature, has been prescribed, and she is even wearing a shawl. How quaint; the look seems a little too 'low' for our widow, but must be the fashion, and sure enough the market for the silk shawls that Spitalfields is suddenly producing is a good one, thank God. And look, after almost eighty years Mrs Jervis has finally decided that she is not Chinese after all, but is drinking her tea from a teacup with a handle

attached to it. Another high game is over; tea drinking is English. Soon we might even see her go out and sit on the grass for a picnic.

But – what is the thread here? Man and Nature in harmony . . . but – what is the idiom? No longer can we look to Rome; we found out too much about it and it now lies so exposed and corrupt that it is coupled in many people's minds with France before the Revolution. So we return to the natural way, as opposed to the un-natural way which we sense is being forced upon us. The human instinct to *purify* is again aroused: the same instinct which once took man out of the clouds and into the Bible, which made us seek to refine our ability to Reason, which has sought the return to purer food and better health. Now it has begun to clean up and strip back Classicism to find its simplest and most original form. For a while – with Napoleon's campaigns – it seemed that Egypt was to be all the rage. However, by being a little bit too exotic, it only succeeded with the mind, but missed with the English heart and failed to align itself to any

243

Christian sentiments. So Greece was thrown the anchor. As we imagine standing before the British Museum, we join in to agree: yes, impressive, perfectly balanced, but set not too high upon a pedestal; no nonsense, no deceptions. Ancient Greece is as pure as were our minds when we were still in the kitchen.

And with another look, so much of Mrs Jervis's little room owes itself to that idiom. The motifs of its furniture and decoration, even its hob grate, as well as the 'feel' created by the sun in this south-facing room, especially when painted in far-away Mediterranean colours. Is this by design?

I begin to think aloud. *'Warmer, less need of a fire – less need of hierarchy – it was the near-naked Greeks and not the fur-coated Siberians who invented Democracy.'* I reach forward and touch Mrs Jervis's new oval-shaped Pembroke tea table. *'The fall of the Ancien Regime was in the name of "Fraternity". One of the claims made against Marie Antoinette at her trial was that she insisted on seating her eldest son at the top end of a rectangular table.'* I leave you to work out the dialogue contained within the Romantic popularity of the rounded rectangle, or *oval*.

'The Elgin Marbles are soon to arrive in England. Imagine an entire culture pictured only in profile!' Looking around, you see that the newer style of chair no longer confronts us head on, as chairs used to, but seeks to persuade us to move around to one side and see people sitting more elegantly, in profile. The whole scene here might best be depicted in the form of a frieze. *'She even sleeps in profile.'* Yes, and so she does.

I explain how the arrival of Mrs Jervis's first grandchildren made her realise how terrifying it might be to a child to have the cold formality of an empty Drawing Room suddenly brought to life by their formidable grandmother, thundering out instructions to her doddering old servants. One day a note appeared in the Drawing Room (still there), which reads, *'Leave things be.'* Relaxed, the furniture

would henceforth remain unarranged, like furniture today, in the position in which it would next be used. When at table, Mrs Jervis surrendered long ago to the 'promiscuous' alternation of the sexes, instead of men at one side and women at the other – as her father-in-law once insisted.

By now I am growing a little suspicious, and allude to the handsome Greek line of Mrs Jervis's black basalt coffee-pot to say: *'Black mourning suits her; don't you think? And, how Nature has won, too . . . see? The stays of her dress have been removed and replaced by the "empire waist" – giving her an outline of, well, undisguised functional femininity. So simple, so Greek; the shape of her less formal day dresses looks just like her teacups, turned upside down.'* I turn one over as an illustration before returning my attention to the coffee-pot. With a turn of my head to one side, I inspect the galleried ridge on top, which contains the lid. *'She wears her hair low and close to the head in "natural" curls and then – I see – uses a headdress of lace to add height.'* Now to the ornament around its base. *'Her shoes are really only just pumps. Nature directly under her feet.'*

I look up to catch sight of you sitting back to look away; you've seen it, but it is – only – a coffee-pot.

From my side of the space between I can feel that I am losing you, and that you have already lost our widow. But so warm, and so comfortable are you now, with no draughts, no shadows and no mystery, that the part of you that once leant to light and warmth – your imagination – is no longer yearning at all.

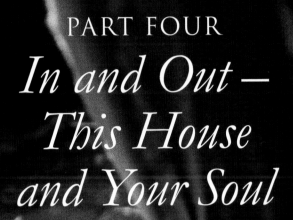

PART FOUR

In and Out —
This House
and Your Soul

CHAPTER NINETEEN

THE SHORT REIGN OF WILLIAM JERVIS

Every once in a while we catch glimpses of young Master William Jervis. The perfect son and heir whom we passed on the Second Half-Landing in the form of a bust, around which were so perfectly arranged his playthings. In his youth he was often said to resemble the young man in the painting *The House of Cards*, by Chardin. ¶ Now grown up, he is not perfect. Agnostic, cynical, suspicious, pretentious, republican – he makes *himself* the centre, but never the end. He takes sides: one minute, One – the next, the Other. His passions rise too high and dive too low whenever he gets cornered. Even more so when he fails to get his own way. Therefore he cannot be trusted and his circle is comprised of the lowest of the high and the highest of the low; 'scum' – as Rebecca calls them. His women are without structure: 'loose' – as Rebecca puts it. With Time his face is becoming more and more difficult to rest the eye on.

Visitor, while under this roof, this man is also *our* son and heir. Our future security will depend on him. What happened to make him so? Were we too busy providing our golden couple with the perfect accessory of a son to attend to the matter of his soul, the core of his being? He was born high up in our adventure, born to sophistication; he did not exist when we were in the kitchen. We took so much care over his parents: to regulate the contentment that gave them their perfect repose. But without a strong centre William has become as vulnerable as are our imaginations; he might, or might not, *do anything.*

It is an evil thing to do: to take a man above the natural level of his place on earth without ensuring that God and Love are alive at his spine. Like the two wings in politics, if the right and left hand are not bonded for the common good, the strong right will drift to greed, while the left will drift towards envy. Looked at scientifically, in William's case – *Up and Down, Back and Forth,* but lacking any *In and Out* – he will have to fall. I should suspect that he, like so many in our own time, will go into whiplash, spasm and then crack.

What can he do? Where can we send him?

Unable to get back *UP,* he began to dive *DOWN* to avoid 'talk' and normal reality, which now seemed too dull in comparison. William was often spotted leaving some of the lowest dens and drinking houses in Clerkenwell at daybreak. These circles were soon to become his own, and though they sought to exploit him for what little he had left, at least they were skilled at knowing how best to make him feel that they believed all his dream-world lies.

Punch bowls, clay pipes, hats worn indoors — and all in the
Drawing Room of our own imaginations! Who are these people?

. . . imagined acquaintances of William — I'm sure; and
brought in by our Heart to speed things up. But now they are
up to mischief, and what of their hangovers, debts — to
say nothing of the mess? . . . what of Tomorrow?
Will Mrs. Jervis's patch box remain behind?

All so easy to fall into for the sake of a thrill, but once started —
have we the faith in our own human structure necessary to draw
things back — not into the opposite extreme, but into a proper line?
Are you quite sure?

In 1825 the Free Trade Act was proposed to Parliament. This was to end Spitalfields' protected monopoly over the silk market at home. The effect was disastrous and the men of the silk trade – many of whom were stunted and hunched by the nature of their work – marched to Westminster to protest. Awestruck Londoners stood at the side to watch on: *'a breed forty years behind the rest of the nation, both physically and mentally'.*

On the morning of the march, William was still involved in the high or low things you like to imagine and did not return from Clerkenwell. The mood in Spitalfields was passionate and a promise had been betrayed. *'That night, the house was set upon by a large hysterical mob. At one point, shots were fired from within the house and over the heads of those outside in order to warn them off. By morning, new shutters were being fitted.'*

As always when under pressure William began to drift, and after disappearing for two days he returned on the morning of the third. A physician was summoned when a fever developed. As the week went on he began to appear distracted and a neighbour discovered him in the street forcing himself to step on each square stone in the street paving. Soon he began to pick at his food. He saw too much – too quickly; and started counting and naming everything in sight. Then he complained that the house was too dark, that it needed light, and that its mystery was threatening his memory. He had to know *everything.* His heart and his conscience suddenly struck back at the inhumanity of his mind: he found himself unable to speak.

I catch your eye and lead it up the stairs to the brooding darkness before I continue. *'On the night of 25 October 1825, when the household thought its master asleep, William Jervis – with nothing to stop him – came unstuck. He hanged himself at the top of the house.'* With a gesture up, I say, *'Up there . . .'* And then, turning my eyes sideways to look directly into yours, I add: *'Too* high? Too *low?* Apparently God's gravity simply will

254

not abide any of that. Thy will be done . . . and the rope snapped! When they found him in the morning, it was right here: lying on this very spot below our feet. That is, at the very centre of this house.'

William had drifted until he went into rigor: a spasm that left his life in ruins. Unlike his parents, whose warmth in a crisis attracted the best of the world, he attracted the worst: those who moved in to bleed him as they picked him clean. The keystone, and the warmth of something at the centre, which were his only prayer, were simply not there.

The Skeleton in the Closet of Our Imaginations

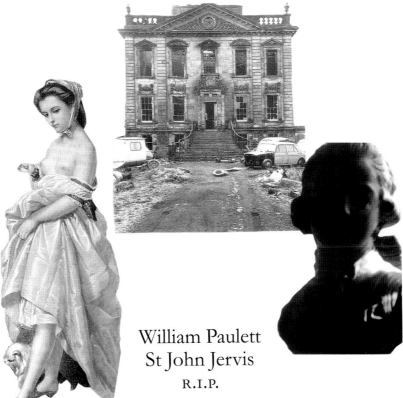

William Paulett
St John Jervis
R.I.P.

Have you ever known anyone who has been thrown out of No. 18? It happens in various ways – sometimes discreetly, but often enough to confirm the legend of my rages and rudeness, of humiliation and heavy-handedness. The reason I make such a fuss at the door is that I can see that it is almost certain to happen later on and I am careful to avoid being paid in advance in case it does. I sense that a visitor has underestimated what is expected, that they have got me confused with a lecturer on local history or interior decoration. No way!

You see, certain regions of Time take a breakdown of both Passions and Reason in order to hurdle their threshold. And Victorian Time, which lies ahead, is one such Time. A Golden Hunch suggests that arrogance and intellectual smugness – including mine – will have to fall. It is not my plot, but that of the Whole Picture. Coming soon, is this house and your Soul.

The nicest and most diplomatic way I have of throwing a visitor out is this. (And for those readers who just love this little pink room, maybe it would be a good idea to close the book at this stage and pretend that you are in South Kensington.) I face the bed and speak:

'Mrs Jervis's bed is 3ft 8in wide, and is 6ft 6in in length. It stands 4ft 2in high, with a mattress height of 1ft 8in. Not authentic to this period, it probably dates from only about c. 1850. English – and not French, as it pretends – it would fetch today between three and four thousand pounds in a salesroom. Sotheby's sold a similar one in 1995 for £6,433. The box springs, and mattress, are both modern, as are the hangings – which are Italian and cost £480 in 1982.'

Sandwiched, suffocated: edged out . . . *murdered* by numbers, names and *compound intelligence*. With nothing left between an old bed and two separated minds, Mrs Jervis is dead. Returned to the golden place from which she was born.

CHAPTER TWENTY

IT WOULD TAKE
A MIRACLE

So, where do we go from here? It would take a miracle to put our imaginations on a new right track now; like it did for old Ebenezer Scrooge in Charles Dickens's classic, *A Christmas Carol.* ¶ Sophie's chamber-stick waits. Surely, not up there! – I push you from behind. Lost, confused, no longer do you trust me or the house, even less so when you hear an alien voice warn from the dark: *'Be careful . . . people up there think and behave without structure . . . might do anything.'* ¶ With each clumsy step – and as I force you up – I speak as I did in earlier times. *'Up to starvation,* up *to leaking ceilings,* up *to damp walls,* up *to cholera and to typhoid. Far up to carefully concealed secrets: to skeletons stored in cupboards, ghosts, and over-crowding. To children and servants kept in attics; to a place with no way of escape, we* rise up in revolution.'

Crushed beneath our feet on each tread are dried crusts of bread, seashells and pieces of broken clay pipes – playthings for children. The lower portions of the walls, at hand level, reflect with the glisten of grease. Dripping from above us we feel the raindrops from wet laundry that could have had little contact with soap. From ahead comes the sound of a silk loom, fitted into a makeshift garret in what was once the Jervises' old attic. All day long: *click, clack – boom! Click, clack – boom!* Like the weavers – or Roman Catholics with their 'Hail Marys', you either develop spiritually or go mad. *Click, clack – boom! Click, clack – boom!* You seem to have forgotten that it was hard, hard work that produced the money which financed the rich existence we once shared with the Jervises.

As we arrive on the top landing I lift the chamber-stick and hold it above your head. I see you sense something, but noticeably you resist looking up, until curiosity gets its way and you lift your gaze to the hook in the ceiling from which William Jervis hanged himself. While staring at you, I reach down and place the light on the floor before the door which opens into the front room. As you prepare to move in that direction – or anywhere to escape me – I surprise you by reaching past you to another door on your left. Now I turn its handle and crack it open. With slow reluctance you turn your head and look over your left shoulder to see what lies within.

Before us now is new ground: *hopeless poverty.* A damp place pregnant with humanity and so awful that it is foul: suffocating air, squalor, with a nest of chairs half-encircling a meagre fire, where cooking and eating in one act have been disturbed by our arrival. Overhead hang more clothes lines, loaded down with literally

everything that needs to be got out of the way. All four corners of the den are packed high with bundles and different sounds suggest the uncomfortable fact that lives of many sorts exist within them.

As you enter, at first you begin to laugh, as so many do, when ideally you should take a deep breath to reach inside yourself and grab on to something that might help you cope. After all, the poor

have to. Instead you go on thinking, and I have to push you on. A baby starts to cry and a hen clucks as we walk forward; someone upstairs in the garret is arguing with someone else, almost to the point of violence. With such unfamiliar coarseness and chaos as distractions, you trip over something lying on the floor and immediately blame it for being in your way.

The ceiling is too low, the panelling has given out on this floor or has been ripped out, like the balustrades on the stairs, and burned as fuel on cold nights. No beginning, no middle, no end. Pictures are hung every which way and the furniture is unarranged; simply pushed to be out of the way. I point at a bed for a crippled child, hidden on the floor under the table to save him from being stepped on, prompted by the same protective instinct as that of a wounded animal. The fire is smouldering with rubbish. Excrement, folded into packets made of newspaper, waits to be hurled out the window into someone else's yard at a time in the night deemed to be *just right*. Everything is – to your mind – wrong. Nothing's right. As we hear the hen squawk again, I prevent you from panicking by assuring you that it is tied to the table by one leg. Whatever it is that you, like the poor, are expected to have inside to catch hold of in order to endure, it is clearly not yet in service. And without structure a bad dream can so easily turn into a nightmare. You are proving to be spoiled, what Rebecca would have described as a 'doughnut' – empty at the centre. I watch your face flash back and forth between Reason and Passion until it actually begins to flush. Robbed of your senses by sophistication and spoiled with *good taste*, *bad taste* has exposed you as inadequate in the face of the real world. Sometimes I fear pushing a visitor too far.

That cry . . . the baby is so obviously sick – I can just imagine you saying to yourself. And, *the smell . . . suffocating.* You squint . . . *that loom; that bloody loom, will it never cease?*

Now I imagine a change in tone. '*This is unfair! Why have you brought me up here? The Jervises would never allow their servants to live like this. This is inaccurate . . . all wrong.*'

My answer to what I imagine is spoken aloud: '*The Jervises? Servants? . . . inaccurate? What would they, or "accuracy", have to do with*

anything real? *This is* our own past, *and no matter how grand either of us thinks we are, from this we come: you are home. And please, no fancy, no Past and no Future.* This *is right now.'*

Your face joins with past visitors to flash a retort, only to find that you cannot. I see you actually contract in size; curiosity and horror make your eyes crawl from one mess to another. To one boiled egg surrounded by waiting crusts of bread. To an unmade bed that looks as if it may house five at a time. To a couple of chairs which marry up to sleep a sixth.

Suddenly all the sounds – in the background all evening – which have kept you as plugged into another time as you are to our own, are – by me – secretly switched off. The silence sends us swirling into an even stronger climate of exposure. And now, instead of sounds around us, we hear one deep, solid voice. It says:

'Remember me? 'Tis I. We were born as one and earlier this evening we were reacquainted in the kitchen, but since then we have been separated – as in Real Life – by your sophistication. And though we have touched near to one another

whenever we have approached the centre of any subject, we are somehow — always kept apart.' We stand in the cold draught of a pause.

The voice continues: *'It is my eternal hope that you will notice that with my presence, what you* like *becomes stronger and more likeable: what you wish well — and hope will survive. That, in my absence, what you* suspect and do not like *— becomes even more suspicious and more unlikeable: it is sometimes what you wish would die. But when at any time you and I join as one, a twinkle comes to your eye and you begin to beam. Such contentment, and its consequences, are my mission. More than light, I am warmth; I am the centre and not the end.'*

Sophie

I reach in front of us and struggle with a chain and a large rusty lock to open the door to the front room: it appears not to have been opened for some time. As the chain drops to the floor, I kick it open, making a cloud of mist lift, before pouring forth, out, sweeping across our faces. The Space Between has returned: it is all around us. At the centre of its mystery is a bed. No, not just *a bed*, but *the very bed* of the aforesaid Mr Ebenezer Scrooge. No more dates or names, no more historical 'accuracy'; to our soul — this is Ebenezer Scrooge's bed. We wish it to be his; and so — we will meet it halfway.

In frosty silence we stand to feel its warmth, and to make the connection: the supernatural has stepped in to foil both mind and heart.

Our new dialogue is *In and Out*, between the soul and its alignment with something greater, outside ourselves; a dialogue that will make what we imagine three-dimensional enough to stand up on its own.

Follow me. We creak past the bed and around into the chamber itself. Once the nursery and servants' bedrooms, now this is a

threadbare and beaten old office. Everywhere we see Dickens: in the shapes of things, his descriptions and characters concealed in the smoky air of all four dark corners.

As we stop before the fire, our eyes go to a chair of miniature proportions meagrely arranged with a tiny footstool and an even tinier cup of tea cupped again by the tiniest of saucers. A cushion completes this very round arrangement, and despite the meanest fire in Great Britain, there is warmth here – despite the fact that everything around it is square, cold and dark. I speak:

'So . . . this is where you keep her: Miss Sophie Jervis.' Down we gawk. 'Kept out on the landings and the stairs – on the other side of keyholes – it is here that she nests. Yes – I see it now. Though her family were the invention of our minds softened by our hearts, willowy and glamorous – Sophie is the residue: the product of the simple soul. All along Sophie has travelled with us to see our over-refinement bring out what is artificial or pretentious . . . she has seen through it all!'

I say aloud to myself, 'Sophie was kept outside, and is therefore still stunted and undeveloped – as souls tend to be. She might easily have embarrassed us by waddling up to kiss and hug us in the Drawing Room – if, that is, she was ever given the chance.' With her two hands pushed into two rounded cheeks, she beams. I add, 'Isolated for so long; at last Sophie – like the rest of her family – finally has a visitor of her own.'

After So Much Time

When in Time, Reason and Romance joined together in the search of a deeper hope, it created a condition called *Victorian*, which derives its name from the fresh image of a diminutive princess.

The memories of the French Revolution, the social nightmares and political turmoil that came with the Industrial Revolution: the move from agriculture to factory production, the rush of the rural poor into hastily built and overcrowded cities. All this, along with the fears of civil disobedience, and new waves of cholera and other diseases, now made Time desperate.

So, what to do? Perhaps it is time for a new tactic. Time to clean things up, Time for Reform,.

This is how it *happens*. This is how it *happened*, and now, this is how it *happens* to you.

Sophie's chamber-stick now begins to sputter its last, and the loss of its flame takes us into total darkness. The light that leads us has, I know, gone indoors. The Space Between is all.

Outside, over the pitched roofs and chimney pots, in the twilight, is the first suggestion of a new dawn. I stand silhouetted between you and London to say, '*Visitor, look. It is the longest day of the year. It is 1837.*'

As I peer out at the peaceful sight, the distant sound of a tolling bell comes to our ears. I turn my head to trace from which direction it travels, only to hear another coming from another direction, followed by another and then another. The house begins to shudder and its window panes rattle, as a blast of artillery fire echoes across the capital. I bend closer to look out and then up, as another is followed by another, and another. I reach over to pick up a newspaper from the seat of the chair before the desk; you watch me check its date. Again I look out into the dawn filling with tolling bells and gunfire. Victoria is Queen.

Everywhere . . . Dickens

'*The house to which Oliver Twist had been conveyed was in the neighbourhood of Whitechapel. It was a very dirty place. The rooms upstairs had great high wooden chimney-pieces and large doors, with panelled walls and cornices to the ceiling: which although they were black with neglect and dust, were ornamental in various*

Oliver asking for more

Fagin in
the condemned Cell

The Last Chance

A Bad
Night

Sikes attempting to destroy his dog

But . . .

ways; from all of which tokens, Oliver concluded, that a long time ago, before Fagin was born, it had belonged to better people, and had perhaps been quite gay and handsome: dismal and dreary as it looked now. Spiders had built their webs in the angles of the walls and ceilings; and sometimes, when Oliver walked softly into a room, the mice would scamper across the floor, and run back terrified to their holes. With these exceptions, there was neither sight nor sound of any living thing . . . alone, he wandered from room to room.'

The heavy blasts of artillery from the great guns at the Tower of London echo across the City as we teeter between our recent despair and this new hope of change. It is the longest day of the year, and I wonder to myself . . . an omen? You stay seated within the pool of darkness at the foot of Scrooge's bed to listen.

Whereas most of the house suggests the Jervises, this room employs a number of images and characters created by Dickens to draw a visitor's imagination outside the house and more generally into the years between 1837 and 1850. More than anywhere else, this – Sophie's Bedroom – holds a visitor closest to the house's motto: *'You either see it or you don't.'* Stripped of any prettiness or warmth, its rawness almost delights in insisting that a visitor turn in and out to anchor what is imagined.

Like the writings of Dickens, sometimes the shadows here can turn from the picturesque to the grotesque in an instant, and over the years many have brought into this room something that has turned on them to make them flee. Some imagine mice and rats; begin picking at their own angles in search of imaginary fleas.

The first but still very faint light reveals that the colour of the Time is, again, brown: somewhere between that evocative foxed-edged parchment and the pen and ink that illustrated the early works of Charles Dickens. Within that twilight hue we look about us to see that we are not alone.

273

'You either see it or you don't'.

Before us on the table sits an empty orphanage gruel bowl from which a wooden spoon projects: *'Please sir, I want some more'?* To one side is an old man's walking stick and a young lady's basket rests upon a crooked chair: Little Nell and Grandfather? Bill Sikes has downed his cudgel to take his last drop; he, like Fagin and the Artful Dodger – with reform so much in the air – must smell their own doom and know that it is time to run.

But working busily behind the small and crooked panes of glass 'tank' – as Dickens called the enclosed clerk's desks of his day

– are others who have nothing to fear: young David Copperfield, Nicholas Nickleby and Bob Cratchit. And is Old Scrooge not behind you in that corner? Still brooding among the cobwebs in that threadbare old armchair. Between his shoes, arranged one on the floor and the other lifted upon a footstool, between his stick, held upright in one hand, and his nightcap sitting, somehow, upon his head? All of us – real or imagined – sit together.

Underneath It All

Once again, Time draws us on. I rise and drift out of the room. I peek past one of the bed curtains to see you staring at Sophie's chamber-stick, still unlit. You carry her light well.

You walk out on the landing among the lines of damp laundry to dodge a threadbare and parchment-coloured shirt.

As, floor by floor we funnel our way down, each door brings back a different set of associations and memories. So too do the cold draughts of the landing and the little patch of fingerprints around each keyhole. Looking back – from here – the whole adventure has finally come together.

I wait for you in the hall, for it was here that we first met a long time ago.

Old Isaac's jacket, wig and tricorne hat hang over the newel post between us – as they have in an odd way all night. Holding your newspaper and umbrella, I take your eye to the front door.

Tick-tock-tick; tick-tock-tick; tick-tock-tick: base, column and capital; a beginning, a middle and an end – and there they go! – all the clocks strike together to bring us home. As old-fashioned and two-dimensional as it might seem to me – here we stand: in **our own Time**.

And, dear visitor, take this as the motto of the house:

AUT VISUM AUT NON!

(Oh, for God's sake!) You either see it or you don't.